MANAGERIAL PSYCHOLOGY

DR.TANMAYA MISHRA

Made with ♥ on the Notion Press Platform
www.notionpress.com

I dedicate this book not only to the world but also to two extraordinary women who have filled my life with boundless love and inspiration.

To my beloved daughter, Ms. Sudiksha Mishra, whose laughter brings joy to my days and whose dreams illuminate my nights. You are my guiding star, my source of pride, and my reason to strive for greatness. May you always chase your dreams fearlessly and walk your chosen path with unwavering determination.

And to my cherished wife, Debjani Mishra, whose unwavering support and unwavering love have been my pillars of strength through every triumph and trial. Your grace, your wisdom, and your boundless kindness enrich my life beyond measure. With you by my side, I am truly blessed, and I am endlessly grateful for the love we share.

This dedication is a token of my deepest love and gratitude to both of you. May our journey together continue to be filled with love, laughter, and countless beautiful memories.

With all my love,

Dr.Tanmaya Kumar Mishra

Contents

Foreword

Preface

Welcome to "Managerial Psychology: Understanding and Harnessing Human Behavior in the Workplace." As an Associate Professor specializing in organizational psychology, my journey into the realms of management and psychology has been both enlightening and rewarding. This book is the culmination of years of research, teaching, and practical experience, aimed at bridging the gap between theory and practice in the field of management.

In today's fast-paced and interconnected world, the success of organizations hinges not only on their products or services but also on the effectiveness of their leadership and management practices. This realization led me to delve deeper into the psychological underpinnings of managerial behavior—the motivations, emotions, and cognitive processes that drive human behavior in organizational settings.

Through this book, my goal is to provide readers with a comprehensive understanding of managerial psychology and equip them with practical tools and strategies to navigate the complexities of modern workplaces. From motivating teams to resolving conflicts, from fostering inclusive cultures to leading change, each chapter explores key concepts and offers actionable insights that can be applied in real-world scenarios.

I invite you to embark on this journey with me—to explore the fascinating intersection of psychology and management, and to discover the transformative power of understanding and harnessing human behavior in the workplace. Whether you are a seasoned manager, a budding leader, or a curious student, I hope that this book inspires you to cultivate empathy, insight, and resilience in your managerial endeavors.

Thank you for joining me on this exploration of managerial psychology. May the insights contained within these pages empower you to lead with purpose, compassion, and effectiveness.

Warm regards,

Dr. Tanmaya Mishra

Acknowledgements

Writing a book is a collaborative endeavor, and I am deeply grateful to the many individuals who have supported and inspired me throughout this journey.

First and foremost, I would like to express my heartfelt gratitude to my colleagues and mentors whose wisdom and guidance have been invaluable. Your encouragement and constructive feedback have shaped this book in profound ways.

I am indebted to the students whose curiosity and enthusiasm continually challenge me to deepen my understanding of managerial psychology. Your passion for learning fuels my own passion for teaching and research.

I extend my sincere appreciation to the staff and administrators at Karnavati University for their unwavering support and dedication to academic excellence.

To my family, friends, and loved ones—thank you for your patience, understanding, and unwavering belief in me. Your love and encouragement have sustained me through the highs and lows of the writing process.

Last but not least, to the readers of this book—thank you for embarking on this journey with me. I hope that the insights shared within these pages empower you to become more effective leaders and managers in your respective fields.

With deepest gratitude,

Dr. Tanmaya Mishra

CHAPTER ONE

Introduction to Managerial Psychology

"Management is doing things right; leadership is doing the right things." — Peter Drucker

This quote by Peter Drucker encapsulates a key principle in managerial psychology: the distinction between the efficient execution of tasks (management) and the strategic, ethical guidance of an organization or team (leadership). It underscores the importance of not only performing tasks correctly but also ensuring that these tasks align with broader goals and values. In the bustling corridors of corporate headquarters, amidst the hum of productivity and the whirl of decision-making, there lies a hidden force—an invisible hand that shapes the fabric of organizations and drives their success. This force is none other than managerial psychology—a field that explores the intricate interplay between human behavior and managerial practices.

Imagine a scenario: Sarah, a manager who's been around the block, steps into a meeting with her team, feeling nervous. The project's due date is getting closer, everyone's on edge, and different tasks are competing for attention. Taking a deep breath, Sarah looks around the room, trying to keep everyone on the same page and feeling like they're part of a team. She knows that how she handles the group's mood could make or break the project, even though it's not something she can see on a chart or in a report.

Managerial psychology, at its core, is the art and science of unraveling the mysteries of human behavior within organizational contexts. It delves into the motivations that drive employees, the emotions that color their interactions, and the cognitive processes that shape their decision-making. By understanding these psychological nuances, managers gain valuable insights into how to effectively lead teams, resolve conflicts, and foster a positive work environment.

Consider another scenario: Alex, a newly appointed team leader, finds herself grappling with a disengaged and unmotivated team. Despite her best efforts to set clear goals and provide feedback, productivity remains stagnant, and morale is at an all-time low. It is only when Alex delves into the principles of motivational psychology—recognizing the importance of autonomy, mastery, and purpose—that she begins to unlock the hidden potential within her team, igniting a spark of enthusiasm and innovation.

Through the lens of managerial psychology, we uncover a world where every managerial decision, every leadership action, is imbued with psychological significance. From the way we communicate and delegate tasks to the way we navigate conflicts and inspire change, our understanding of human behavior shapes the very fabric of organizational culture and performance.

In this book, we embark on a journey into the heart of managerial psychology—a journey that explores the fascinating interplay between psychology and management, and the profound implications for leadership and organizational success. Through captivating examples, practical insights, and thought-provoking discussions, we unravel the mysteries of human behavior in the workplace, empowering managers to lead with empathy, insight, and effectiveness.

Join me as we delve into the captivating world of managerial psychology—a world where the power of understanding human behavior transforms managers into leaders, and organizations into thriving ecosystems of productivity and innovation.

Definition and Scope of Managerial Psychology

Managerial psychology is a multidisciplinary field that examines the psychological principles underlying managerial behavior and organizational dynamics. At its core, it seeks to understand how human cognition, emotions, and motivations influence managerial decision-making, leadership effectiveness, and workplace dynamics.

The scope of managerial psychology encompasses a wide range of topics, including:

- ***Motivation and Engagement:*** *Exploring the factors that drive employee motivation, such as intrinsic rewards, goal-setting, and job satisfaction. Understanding how to cultivate a work environment that fosters engagement and commitment.*
- ***Leadership and Influence:*** *Investigating different leadership styles and their impact on employee performance and organizational outcomes. Examining the role of emotional intelligence, charisma, and persuasion in effective leadership.*

- ***Communication and Conflict Resolution:*** *Studying communication patterns within organizations and how they affect collaboration, team dynamics, and conflict resolution. Identifying strategies for fostering open communication, active listening, and constructive feedback.*

- ***Decision-Making and Problem-Solving:*** *Analyzing the cognitive processes involved in managerial decision-making, including biases, heuristics, and risk perception. Developing frameworks for effective problem-solving and decision-making under uncertainty.*

- ***Organizational Culture and Change Management:*** *Exploring the role of culture in shaping organizational norms, values, and practices. Examining strategies for managing organizational change, overcoming resistance, and fostering a culture of innovation.*

- ***Team Dynamics and Collaboration:*** *Understanding the psychological dynamics of teamwork, including group cohesion, role clarity, and conflict resolution. Identifying strategies for building high-performing teams and promoting collaboration.*

- ***Employee Well-being and Work-Life Balance:*** *Investigating the impact of work-related stress, burnout, and work-life balance on employee performance and organizational outcomes. Developing strategies for promoting employee well-being and resilience.*

Managerial psychology draws from various disciplines, including psychology, organizational behavior, sociology, and management theory. It provides managers with valuable insights and practical tools for navigating the complexities of the modern workplace, fostering a culture of trust, engagement, and innovation. Ultimately, managerial psychology seeks to empower managers to lead with empathy, insight, and effectiveness, driving organizational success while prioritizing the well-being and satisfaction of employees.

Importance of Managerial Psychology in the Modern Workplace

In today's rapidly evolving business landscape, the importance of managerial psychology cannot be overstated. As organizations strive to adapt to technological advancements, shifting market trends, and diverse workforce demographics, effective leadership and management practices have become more crucial than ever. Here are several reasons why managerial psychology is indispensable in the modern workplace:

- ***Understanding Employee Motivation:*** *Managerial psychology helps leaders understand the underlying motivations that drive employee behavior. By recognizing individual differences in motivation and tailoring strategies accordingly, managers can cultivate a motivated and engaged workforce, leading to higher levels of productivity and job satisfaction.*

- ***Enhancing Communication and Collaboration:*** *Effective communication is essential for fostering collaboration, resolving conflicts, and building strong relationships within teams. Managerial psychology provides insights into communication styles, barriers to effective communication, and strategies for improving interpersonal interactions, thereby promoting a culture of trust, transparency, and mutual respect.*

- ***Optimizing Decision-Making Processes:*** *In today's fast-paced business environment, managers are often required to make decisions under uncertainty and time constraints. Managerial psychology offers frameworks for understanding decision-making biases, heuristics, and cognitive limitations, enabling managers to make more informed and effective decisions that align with organizational goals.*

- ***Promoting Leadership Effectiveness:*** *Leadership is a critical factor in driving organizational performance and employee engagement. Managerial psychology helps leaders develop self-awareness, emotional intelligence, and effective leadership styles that inspire and empower their teams. By cultivating strong leadership capabilities, organizations can navigate change, foster innovation, and achieve sustainable growth.*

- ***Managing Organizational Change:*** *In an era of constant disruption and transformation, the ability to manage change effectively is paramount. Managerial psychology provides insights into the psychological processes involved in change, including resistance to change, fear of uncertainty, and the importance of communication and employee involvement. Armed with this knowledge, managers can implement change initiatives with greater success and minimize resistance.*

- ***Promoting Employee Well-being:*** *Employee well-being is not only a moral imperative but also a strategic advantage for organizations. Managerial psychology emphasizes the importance of creating a supportive work environment, promoting work-life balance, and addressing factors that contribute to stress and burnout. By prioritizing employee well-being, organizations can enhance retention rates, attract top talent, and foster a culture of innovation and creativity.*

Aspect of Managerial Psychology	Key Points
Understanding Employee Motivation	Recognizing individual differences in motivation; Tailoring motivational strategies to align with employee needs and preferences
Enhancing Communication and Collaboration	Understanding communication styles and preferences; Overcoming barriers to effective communication; Fostering a culture of open communication
Optimizing Decision-Making Processes	Identifying decision-making biases and cognitive limitations; Using decision-making frameworks to make informed and effective decisions
Promoting Leadership Effectiveness	Developing self-awareness and emotional intelligence; Cultivating effective leadership styles that inspire and empower teams
Managing Organizational Change	Understanding psychological processes involved in change; Addressing resistance to change; Communicating change effectively to stakeholders
Promoting Employee Well-being	Creating a supportive work environment; Promoting work-life balance; Addressing factors contributing to stress and burnout

These key points highlight the diverse aspects of managerial psychology and the importance of each in fostering a positive work environment and driving organizational success.

Overview of Key Concepts in Managerial Psychology

Managerial psychology encompasses a variety of key concepts that are essential for understanding human behavior in organizational settings and guiding effective management practices. Here's a brief overview of some of these fundamental concepts:

- *Motivation: Understanding what drives individuals to perform their best at work. This includes intrinsic motivators like personal growth and achievement, as well as extrinsic motivators like rewards and recognition.*

- *Leadership Styles: Exploring different approaches to leadership and their impact on employee performance and organizational culture. This includes transformational, transactional, and servant leadership styles, among others.*

-

Communication: Recognizing the importance of clear and effective communication in fostering collaboration, resolving conflicts, and building trust within teams and across organizational hierarchies.

- *Decision-Making: Analyzing the cognitive processes involved in decision-making and identifying factors that influence choices, such as biases, heuristics, and risk perception.*

- *Emotional Intelligence: Developing awareness and understanding of one's own emotions and those of others, and using this knowledge to navigate interpersonal relationships and lead with empathy and authenticity.*

- *Organizational Culture: Examining the shared values, beliefs, and norms that shape behavior within an organization, and understanding how culture influences employee engagement, performance, and satisfaction.*

- *Change Management: Implementing strategies to effectively manage organizational change, including communicating the need for change, engaging employees in the process, and overcoming resistance to new initiatives.*

- *Team Dynamics: Understanding the dynamics of group behavior, including communication patterns, role clarity, and conflict resolution strategies, and fostering high-performing teams that achieve collective goals.*

- *Employee Well-being: Prioritizing the physical, emotional, and psychological well-being of employees, and implementing policies and practices that promote work-life balance, reduce stress, and enhance job satisfaction.*

- *Performance Management: Establishing systems for setting goals, providing feedback, and evaluating employee performance, with the aim of improving individual and organizational effectiveness.*

These key concepts form the foundation of managerial psychology, providing managers with a framework for understanding and addressing the complexities of human behavior in the workplace. By applying these concepts effectively, managers can enhance employee engagement, foster a positive organizational culture, and drive sustainable performance and growth.

Aspect	Managerial Psychology	Industrial Psychology
Definition	Focuses on understanding, predicting, and influencing managerial behavior within organizations.	Focuses on the scientific study of human behavior in the workplace and applies psychological theories to improve employee performance and well-being.
Scope	Deals with leadership, motivation, decision-making, and team dynamics.	Encompasses recruitment, selection, training, performance appraisal, and occupational health and safety.
Primary Objectives	Enhance managerial effectiveness and leadership skills.	Optimize human resource functions and improve workplace efficiency and employee satisfaction.
Key Topics	Leadership styles, emotional intelligence, motivation theories, conflict resolution.	Job analysis, employee selection, training development, performance management, ergonomics.
Research Methods	Case studies, surveys, behavioral assessments, organizational simulations.	Psychological testing, experimental studies, field studies, surveys.
Application Examples	- Developing leadership training programs to enhance managerial skills - Implementing motivational strategies to improve team performance.	- Designing effective recruitment and selection processes. - Creating training programs to enhance employee skills and productivity.
Research Facts	- Studies show that managers with high emotional intelligence lead more effective teams (Goleman, 1998). E11Effective decision-making in managers is linked to better organizational outcomes (Kahneman, 2011).	- Structured interviews are more reliable predictors of job performance than unstructured ones (Hunter & Hunter, 1984).E8 - Employee training programs significantly improve job performance and job satisfaction (Arthur et al., 2003).
Historical Development	Emerged from organizational behavior and leadership studies in the mid-20th century.	Originated from the early 20th-century study of industrial efficiency and worker productivity (Taylorism).
Theoretical Frameworks	- Maslow's Hierarchy of Needs - Herzberg's Two-Factor Theory - Vroom's Expectancy Theory	- Taylor's Scientific Management - Hawthorne Studies - Theory of Work Adjustment
Practical Impact	Improves managerial practices and leadership effectiveness, leading to better team performance and organizational success.	Enhances employee selection, training, and workplace conditions, leading to higher productivity and employee satisfaction.

Difference Between Managerial Psychology and Industrial Psychology

Research Facts and Examples

Industrial Psychology:

Example: A tech company revises its recruitment process to include structured interviews and job simulations. This change leads to improved new hire performance and decreased time-to-hire.

Research Fact: Structured interviews are more reliable predictors of job performance than unstructured interviews (Hunter & Hunter, 1984).

Managerial Psychology:

Example: A multinational company implements an emotional intelligence training program for its managers, resulting in increased team productivity and reduced employee turnover.

Research Fact: Leaders with high emotional intelligence significantly outperform their peers, showing better team cohesion and performance (Goleman, 1998).

While industrial psychology focuses broadly on optimizing workplace conditions and improving employee performance through effective HR practices and workplace design, managerial psychology zeroes in on enhancing the behavior, skills, and effectiveness of managers and leaders within organizations. Both fields are essential for fostering a productive and satisfying work environment, but they address different aspects of organizational life. Understanding their distinctions and interconnections can help organizations leverage the strengths of both to achieve comprehensive improvements.

Key Theoretical Ideas in Contemporary Psychological Theory and Practice

Consider three key theoretical ideas prevalent in contemporary psychological theory and practice: motivation, reinforcement, and cognition.

Motivation

Motivation revolves around people's drives, needs, and desires. It includes the internal tensions that propel individuals to seek out both straightforward needs like food and shelter and more complex desires like love, achievement, and personal fulfillment. Most theories about motivation explore the dynamics of human personality and potential. For instance, a hungry person searches for food, driven by the tension of hunger. Similarly, individuals strive for achievements driven by internal desires for success and recognition.

Reinforcement

Reinforcement involves the use of rewards and punishments, primarily from external sources, to shape behavior. The idea of reinforcement is grounded in learning theories like the "law of effect," which states that behaviors followed by satisfying outcomes are likely to be repeated. For example, if a child receives praise for completing homework, they are more likely to do it again. Reinforcement is crucial because it directs human behavior by encouraging the repetition of actions that lead to positive outcomes.

Cognition

Cognition encompasses thinking, anticipating, and learning from others' experiences. It involves the mind's ability to imagine, expect, estimate, and generalize. For example, if someone observes a colleague being rewarded for a particular behavior, they might anticipate similar rewards for themselves and act accordingly. Cognition adds depth to our understanding of human behavior by recognizing that people don't just act based on reinforcement but also think about their actions and outcomes, making deliberate choices.

Integration and Application

These three concepts—motivation, reinforcement, and cognition—apply universally to everyone. We all have motivations, respond to reinforcement, and engage in cognitive processes. Treating these ideas as gateways to understanding human complexity helps explain behavior. For example, motivation theories often stem from Freudian psychoanalytic thinking, viewing humans as driven by internal tensions seeking fulfillment. Reinforcement theory, derived from the work of Pavlov, Watson, and Skinner, sees humans as learning through rewards and punishments. Finally, cognition theory acknowledges that humans think, learn from others, and anticipate outcomes, adding a layer of complexity to our understanding of behavior.

Example of Application

In the workplace, managers can use these theories to improve employee performance and satisfaction. For instance, understanding motivation can help managers design tasks that fulfill employees' needs for achievement and recognition. Utilizing reinforcement can shape desired behaviors through rewards like bonuses or praise. Encouraging cognitive processes can foster innovation and problem-solving by allowing employees to learn from each other and anticipate future challenges.

By combining these concepts, managers can create a more comprehensive approach to understanding and influencing employee behavior, leading to a more motivated, skilled, and proactive workforce.

Historical Development of Managerial Psychology

The field of managerial psychology emerged in the early 20th century, significantly influenced by several pioneering psychologists who laid the groundwork for what is now known as industrial and organizational (I/O) psychology. These foundational figures included James Cattell, Hugo Münsterberg, Walter Dill Scott, and Lillian Gilbreth. James Cattell, the founder of the Psychological Corporation, established a lasting legacy in psychological consulting that continues today. Hugo Münsterberg's seminal work, Psychology and Industrial Efficiency (1913), explored critical areas such as employee selection, training, and effective advertising. Walter Dill Scott was among the first to apply psychological principles to advertising, management, and personnel selection, as documented in his influential books The Theory of Advertising and Psychology of Advertising. Lillian Gilbreth made significant contributions through her work on time and motion studies, efficiency, and human factors. These early psychologists not only held academic positions but also directly consulted with businesses, laying a solid foundation for industrial and organizational psychology.

The involvement of psychologists in World War I marked a significant turning point in the application of psychological principles to real-world problems, particularly within the military. Robert Yerkes, under the Surgeon General's Office (SGO), organized efforts to develop methods for screening and selecting enlisted men, leading to the creation of the Army Alpha test to measure mental abilities. Similarly, Walter Bingham and Walter Dill Scott formed a group under the Adjutant General's Office (AGO) to develop selection methods for officers. This period saw a primary focus on what is now recognized as industrial psychology, which involved the practical application of psychological methods to enhance efficiency and performance in industrial settings. The involvement in the war effort demonstrated the practical value of psychology and set the stage for its future applications in various organizational contexts.

The maturation and expansion of industrial psychology continued throughout the early to mid-20th century. The influential Hawthorne Studies, conducted between 1920 and 1939, were pivotal in understanding the social and psychological aspects of work environments and employee productivity. These studies highlighted the importance of considering human relations and the social context in which work occurs. During World War II, the field expanded significantly due to the increased demand for psychological expertise in personnel selection, training, and morale. The post-war period saw industrial psychology mature further, incorporating insights from various psychological disciplines to address complex organizational issues.

By the 1960s and 1970s, the field had evolved to encompass a broader focus, leading to the adoption of the term "industrial-organizational psychology." This new designation reflected an expanded scope that included not only traditional areas such as personnel selection and training but also emerging areas like organizational behavior, leadership, and human resources management. The broader focus allowed I/O psychologists to address a wider range of issues within organizations, from enhancing individual performance to improving organizational culture and leadership practices. This period also saw increased professionalization and the establishment of I/O psychology as a distinct discipline within psychology.

Today, industrial-organizational psychology continues to evolve, integrating advances in technology, data analytics, and understanding of human behavior to address contemporary organizational challenges. The foundational work of early pioneers like Cattell, Münsterberg, Scott, and Gilbreth remains influential, providing a historical context for ongoing developments in the field. Modern I/O psychologists build on this legacy, applying scientific methods to solve practical problems in the workplace, enhancing employee well-being, and improving organizational effectiveness. The field's evolution from its early 20th-century origins to its current status underscores the enduring importance of psychological insights in understanding and optimizing human behavior within organizational settings.

Recent Trends in Managerial Psychology

Equity, Diversity, and Inclusion (EDI) have become crucial areas of focus for organizations worldwide. As the demand for leadership in these areas grows, psychologists are playing a significant role in addressing these important issues within workplaces. Organizations are starting to understand the value of creating inclusive environments where diverse perspectives are respected and equal opportunities are provided for all employees. This shift towards equity, diversity, and inclusion is not just a moral imperative but also beneficial for the overall success and innovation within organizations.

In recent years, there has been a significant change in how organizations view employee mental health. Psychologists are leading efforts to help businesses prioritize the well-being of their workers. Companies are increasingly investing in wellness programs, stress management techniques, and work-life balance initiatives. These efforts are designed to support the overall mental and physical health of employees, recognizing that a healthy workforce is more productive and engaged.

The Covid-19 pandemic brought about unprecedented challenges, affecting employees, teams, and organizations around the world. The disruption caused by the pandemic has led researchers to study its impact on management and organizational behavior extensively. These studies provide valuable insights into how organizations can manage through future crises or any large-scale disruptions. Learning from the pandemic, businesses are better prepared to handle similar events in the future, ensuring the resilience and adaptability of their operations.

Advancements in behavioral science and neuroscience over the past twenty years have greatly influenced our understanding of managerial decision-making. Researchers are using new tools and theories to explore how managers make choices, lead teams, and handle complex organizational issues. These scientific advancements help us understand the underlying processes that drive managerial behavior, leading to more effective leadership strategies and improved organizational performance.

Overall, the integration of equity, diversity, and inclusion, the prioritization of worker well-being, the lessons learned from the Covid-19 pandemic, and the advancements in behavioral science and neuroscience are shaping the future of organizational management. These elements highlight the importance of a holistic approach to managing people and organizations, focusing not only on productivity but also on creating supportive and inclusive environments where everyone can thrive.

The implementation of Equity, Diversity, and Inclusion (EDI) in organizations goes beyond just moral and ethical considerations; it also positively impacts business outcomes. Studies have shown that companies with diverse workforces are more innovative and better at problem-solving due to the variety of perspectives and ideas brought by employees from different backgrounds. For example, a 2018 McKinsey report found that organizations in the top quartile for gender diversity on executive teams were 21% more likely to outperform on profitability and 27% more likely to have superior value creation. Similarly, those in the top quartile for ethnic and cultural diversity were 33% more likely to have industry-leading profitability. These statistics underscore the tangible benefits of fostering an inclusive environment that values diversity.

Worker well-being has become a central focus for many organizations, particularly in light of growing awareness around mental health issues. According to the American Psychological Association (APA), workplaces that invest in mental health support see a reduction in absenteeism, higher employee engagement, and improved productivity. Companies like Google and Microsoft have set examples by offering comprehensive wellness programs that include mental health days, access to counseling services, and mindfulness training. For instance, Google's "gPause" program encourages employees to incorporate mindfulness into their daily routines, which has been shown to reduce stress and enhance overall well-being. These initiatives not only benefit employees but also contribute to a more motivated and efficient workforce.

The Covid-19 pandemic forced organizations to rapidly adapt to new ways of working, with remote work becoming the norm for many. This shift highlighted the importance of flexibility and resilience in management practices. Research conducted by the Harvard Business Review indicates that companies with strong crisis management plans and adaptive leadership were better able to navigate the challenges posed by the pandemic. For example, companies like Twitter and Shopify quickly implemented remote work policies and provided employees with the necessary tools and support to work from home effectively. These companies also prioritized clear communication and mental health support during the transition, which helped maintain productivity and employee morale. The lessons learned from the pandemic underscore the need for agile and responsive management strategies that can handle unexpected disruptions.

In conclusion, the focus on EDI, worker well-being, and adaptive management strategies are reshaping how organizations operate. The evidence and examples from leading companies demonstrate that prioritizing these areas not only fosters a healthier and more inclusive work environment but also drives business success. As organizations continue to evolve, integrating these principles into their core strategies will be crucial for long-term sustainability and growth.

Questions:

1. *What is managerial psychology, and why is it important in the context of organizational management?*
2. *How does understanding human behavior contribute to effective management practices?*
3. *What are some key areas of focus within the scope of managerial psychology?*
4. *How does an understanding of managerial psychology contribute to building high-performing teams?*
5. *What role does communication play in shaping organizational culture and fostering collaboration?*
6. *What are some common challenges managers face in leadership roles, and how can managerial psychology help address these challenges?*

CHAPTER TWO

The Psychology of Motivation

"People often say that motivation doesn't last. Well, neither does bathing – that's why we recommend it daily." — Zig Ziglar

This quote by Zig Ziglar emphasizes the necessity of consistently renewing and maintaining motivation. It suggests that motivation is not a one-time effort but a continual process that needs regular reinforcement, much like other daily habits essential for well-being. Motivation is the driving force behind human behavior, encompassing the psychological processes that initiate, direct, and sustain goal-oriented actions. At its core, motivation involves the interplay of internal factors, such as personal goals, values, and beliefs, and external factors, such as rewards, recognition, and social influences. It is a dynamic process that can fluctuate in response to changing circumstances and individual experiences. Motivation fuels individuals to pursue desired outcomes, overcome obstacles, and strive for excellence in various aspects of their lives.

In the corporate world, motivation plays a pivotal role in shaping employee performance, job satisfaction, and organizational success. Effective leaders and managers understand the importance of cultivating a motivated workforce and employ various strategies to harness individuals‘ intrinsic and extrinsic motivators. This may include providing clear goals and expectations, offering opportunities for skill development and career advancement, fostering a supportive work environment, and recognizing and rewarding achievements. By aligning organizational objectives with individual aspirations and values, leaders can inspire commitment, engagement, and discretionary effort among employees, driving productivity and innovation within the organization.

Leaders and managers also play a crucial role in motivating clients and customers, whether through product innovation, exceptional service delivery, or personalized attention. By understanding clients' needs, preferences, and motivations, leaders can tailor their offerings to meet and exceed expectations, building trust, loyalty, and long-term relationships. Effective communication, responsiveness, and empathy are key to fostering positive client experiences and cultivating a sense of partnership and mutual benefit. Ultimately, leaders who prioritize client satisfaction and strive to add value to their client's lives are more likely to succeed in today's competitive marketplace.

Theories of Motivation

Motivation, often defined as the inner drive that prompts individuals to take certain actions or pursue specific goals, lies at the heart of managerial psychology. Whether it's completing a task, achieving a goal, or striving for personal growth, motivation shapes how individuals approach their work and interact within organizational settings. By understanding the theories of motivation, managers can unlock the potential of their teams, foster a culture of engagement, and drive sustainable performance.

1. Maslow's Hierarchy of Needs

Abraham Maslow's Hierarchy of Needs theory posits that human needs can be arranged into a hierarchical structure, with lower-order needs (such as physiological and safety needs) forming the foundation, and higher-order needs (such as esteem and self-actualization) situated at the pinnacle. Maslow argued that individuals are motivated to fulfill their basic needs before progressing to higher levels of psychological growth and fulfillment. Corporate Example: Companies can recognize Maslow's theory by providing employees with competitive salaries (addressing physiological needs), opportunities for career advancement (fulfilling esteem needs), and initiatives for personal development and self-expression (nurturing self-actualization needs).

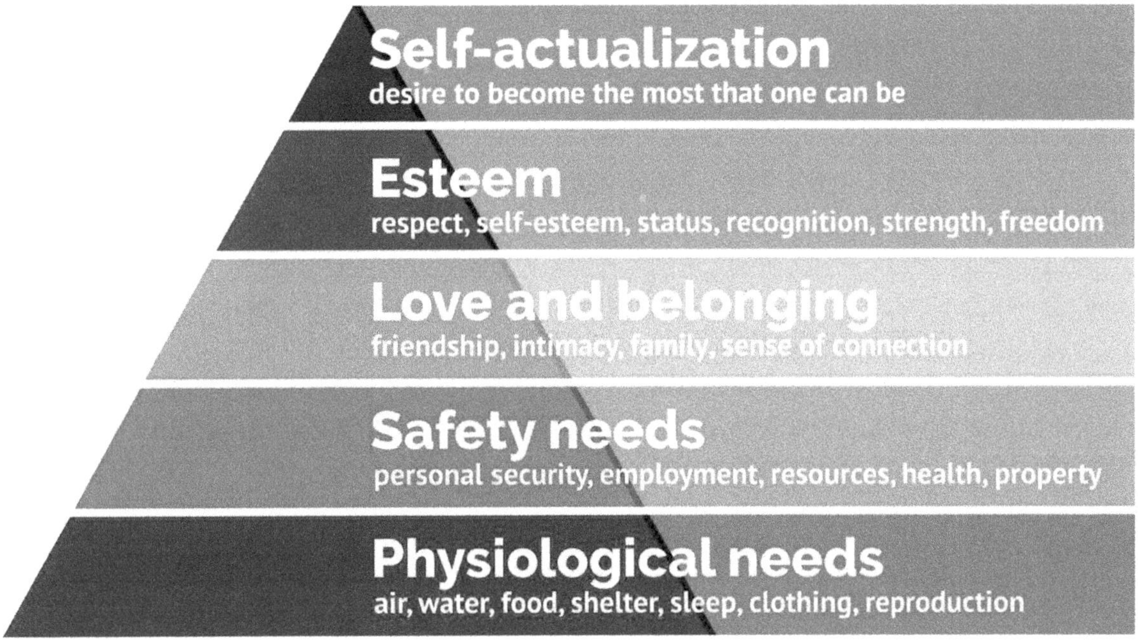

Self-actualization
desire to become the most that one can be

Esteem
respect, self-esteem, status, recognition, strength, freedom

Love and belonging
friendship, intimacy, family, sense of connection

Safety needs
personal security, employment, resources, health, property

Physiological needs
air, water, food, shelter, sleep, clothing, reproduction

Maslow's hierarchy of needs

2. Herzberg's Two-Factor Theory

Frederick Herzberg's Two-Factor Theory distinguishes between hygiene factors and motivators in the workplace. Hygiene factors, such as working conditions and salary, are essential for preventing dissatisfaction but do not necessarily lead to higher motivation. In contrast, motivators, such as recognition and opportunities for growth, are intrinsic factors that directly contribute to job satisfaction and motivation. Corporate Example: Companies can focus on improving hygiene factors like workplace safety and fair compensation to prevent dissatisfaction among employees, while also implementing motivators like recognition programs and opportunities for career advancement to enhance job satisfaction and motivation.

3. Expectancy Theory

Victor Vroom's Expectancy Theory suggests that individuals are motivated to act in a certain way based on their belief that their efforts will lead to desired outcomes, and that these outcomes are valuable to them. The theory emphasizes the importance of expectancy (belief that effort will lead to performance), instrumentality (belief that performance will lead to outcomes), and valence (value of outcomes) in shaping motivation. Corporate Example: An employee may be motivated to work harder on a project if they believe that their efforts will result in a promotion (high expectancy), and that the promotion will lead to increased job satisfaction and financial rewards (positive valence).

4. Goal-Setting Theory

Goal-Setting Theory, pioneered by Edwin Locke and Gary Latham, emphasizes the importance of setting specific and challenging goals to enhance motivation and performance. Clear goals provide direction, enhance focus, and increase persistence, leading to improved task performance and job satisfaction. Corporate Example: A sales team may set specific and challenging targets for revenue generation, encouraging employees to strive for excellence and surpass their previous performance. Regular feedback and recognition of progress towards these goals can further motivate employees to achieve success.

5. Self-Determination Theory

Self-Determination Theory, developed by Edward Deci and Richard Ryan, posits that individuals are motivated by three innate psychological needs: autonomy (the desire to have control over one's actions), competence (the desire to feel capable and effective), and relatedness (the desire to feel connected to others). Fulfilling these basic needs promotes intrinsic motivation and fosters engagement and well-being in the workplace. Corporate Example: A company may foster employee motivation by providing opportunities for autonomy, such as flexible work hours or the ability to choose projects. Additionally, creating a supportive and inclusive work environment can fulfill employees' need for relatedness, enhancing their overall motivation and engagement.

6. X and Y Theory

X and Y theory, proposed by Douglas McGregor, offers contrasting views on employee motivation and management philosophy. In Theory X, managers assume that employees are inherently lazy, dislike work, and require constant supervision and control to perform effectively. This theory advocates for a directive and authoritarian management style, where managers use coercion, punishment, and strict oversight to ensure compliance and productivity. In contrast, Theory Y posits that employees are inherently motivated, responsible, and capable of self-direction and self-control. According to Theory Y, managers should adopt a participative and empowering leadership approach, providing opportunities for autonomy, creativity, and personal growth. By trusting and empowering employees, Theory Y managers believe they can unlock the full potential of their workforce, fostering innovation, commitment, and organizational success.

7. Integrating Motivational Theories in Practice

In practice, effective managers leverage a combination of motivational theories to create environments where employees feel valued, engaged, and motivated to perform at their best. By understanding the diverse needs and preferences of their team members, managers can tailor motivational strategies to enhance job satisfaction, drive performance, and promote organizational success. Through recognition programs, opportunities for skill development, and a supportive work culture, managers can cultivate a motivated and high-performing workforce that propels the organization towards its goals.

Intrinsic and Extrinsic Motivation

Intrinsic and extrinsic motivation represent two distinct sources of drive and behavior in individuals. Intrinsic motivation arises from internal factors, such as personal interest, enjoyment, or satisfaction derived from performing an activity or achieving a goal. It is driven by the inherent pleasure and fulfillment associated with the task itself, rather than external rewards or incentives. In contrast, extrinsic motivation stems from external factors, such as rewards, recognition, or avoidance of punishment. Individuals who are extrinsically motivated are influenced by tangible outcomes or consequences, seeking to attain rewards or avoid negative outcomes. While both forms of motivation play important roles in shaping behavior, intrinsic motivation is often associated with higher levels of engagement, creativity, and long-term satisfaction, as it reflects genuine interest and personal fulfillment in the task at hand.

Aspect	Intrinsic Motivation	Extrinsic Motivation
Source	Arises from internal factors, such as personal interest, enjoyment, or satisfaction derived from the activity itself.	Stem from external factors, such as rewards, recognition, or avoidance of punishment.
Focus	Driven by the inherent pleasure and fulfillment associated with the task or goal.	Influenced by tangible outcomes or consequences, seeking to attain rewards or avoid negative outcomes.
Examples	Pursuing a hobby out of genuine interest and passion.	Completing a task to earn a bonus or avoid disciplinary action.
Sustainability	Often leads to sustained engagement, creativity, and satisfaction over the long term.	May lead to short-term compliance or performance but may not foster intrinsic enjoyment or commitment.
Impact on Behavior	Associated with higher levels of autonomy, creativity, and self-determination.	May result in task completion or goal achievement driven by external incentives.

The difference between intrinsic and extrinsic motivation

Strategies to motivate employees

Motivating employees effectively requires a combination of recognition, career development opportunities, and a healthy work-life balance. Regularly recognizing and rewarding employees' achievements, both publicly and privately, can significantly boost morale and motivation. This can include monetary rewards like bonuses or raises, as well as non-monetary rewards such as extra vacation days or personalized thank-you notes. Additionally, providing career development opportunities through training programs, mentorship, and clear career pathing helps employees feel valued and invested in their future within the company.

Creating an engaging work environment is also crucial for motivation. Fostering an inclusive culture where diversity is celebrated ensures that all employees feel respected and valued. Team-building activities and social events can strengthen team cohesion and camaraderie, while involving employees in decision-making processes encourages a sense of ownership and engagement. Furthermore, setting SMART goals (Specific, Measurable, Achievable, Relevant, and Time-bound) provides clear direction and purpose, and regular feedback helps employees understand their progress and areas for improvement.

Finally, promoting work-life balance and empowering employees with autonomy are essential strategies for maintaining motivation. Flexible scheduling, remote work options, and wellness programs help employees manage their personal and professional lives better, reducing burnout and enhancing productivity. Trusting employees with meaningful tasks and giving them the autonomy to make decisions in their roles fosters a sense of responsibility and ownership. By combining these strategies, managers can create a motivating environment that supports both individual growth and organizational success.

Mind: Thinking, Creating, Analyzing

The human mind is a powerful tool capable of remarkable feats in thinking, creating, and analyzing. These cognitive abilities form the backbone of innovation and problem-solving in various fields. For instance, in the technology sector, the process of thinking and analyzing is crucial in developing new software and algorithms. Take Google's DeepMind, which created AlphaGo, the first computer program to defeat a world champion at the game of Go. This achievement was a result of advanced analytical thinking and creative problem-solving, where the team behind AlphaGo combined deep learning and neural network techniques to develop a system that could learn and adapt in ways previously thought impossible for artificial intelligence. Such examples highlight how analytical thinking and creativity are intertwined, driving progress and breakthroughs in complex domains.

In the realm of art and literature, the creative power of the mind is vividly demonstrated through the works of renowned individuals who push the boundaries of human imagination. Consider J.K. Rowling, whose Harry Potter series has captivated millions worldwide. Her ability to think creatively and construct a detailed, magical world with intricate plots and rich characters showcases the incredible potential of the human mind in storytelling. Similarly, in the field of design and architecture, the work of Frank Lloyd Wright exemplifies the creative and analytical capabilities of the mind. Wright's innovative designs, such as the Fallingwater house, integrate natural landscapes with architectural form, demonstrating a profound understanding of both artistic creativity and structural analysis. These examples illustrate that the mind's ability to think, create, and analyze not only fuels individual achievements but also contributes significantly to cultural and technological advancements.

Cognitive processes drive creativity, problem-solving, and decision-making. We explore how managers think, create, and analyze information.

***John R. Hayes's "Cognitive Processes in Creative Acts"** delves into how our minds work during the creative process, exploring the mental steps involved in generating new ideas and solutions. Hayes argues that creativity isn't just a spontaneous burst of inspiration but involves structured thinking, problem-solving, and the ability to connect disparate concepts in novel ways. For instance, in professional settings, a marketing team might use brainstorming sessions to come up with a new campaign. This process involves examining current trends, understanding customer needs, and blending various ideas to create an innovative strategy. Similarly, in engineering, a team might face a technical challenge and use creative problem-solving techniques to design a new product. By breaking down the problem, analyzing possible solutions, and thinking outside the box, they can develop a unique and effective solution. These examples illustrate how understanding the cognitive processes behind creativity can enhance innovation and effectiveness in professional life.*

***James L. Adams's "Emotional Blocks"** focuses on how emotions can hinder creative thinking, emphasizing that overcoming these barriers is crucial for innovation. Adams* *identifies several emotional blocks, such as fear of failure, self-doubt, and the desire for conformity, which can prevent individuals from exploring new ideas or taking risks. For example, in a professional setting, a software development team might be hesitant to suggest a novel approach to a project due to fear of criticism or failure. This emotional block can stifle innovation and limit the team's potential. Similarly, in a corporate environment, employees might avoid proposing bold strategies if they feel their ideas won't be accepted or valued by their peers or superiors. By recognizing and addressing these emotional barriers, organizations can create a more supportive environment that encourages creative thinking and allows for more groundbreaking ideas to emerge. This understanding helps teams to be more open, take calculated risks, and ultimately drive innovation.*

Charles E. Lindblom's "The Science of 'Muddling Through'" *presents a pragmatic approach to decision-making in complex situations, emphasizing incremental steps over grand, sweeping reforms. Lindblom argues that in the face of complexity and uncertainty, small, manageable adjustments are more effective and practical than attempting to overhaul systems entirely. This method, known as incrementalism, allows for continuous learning and adaptation as each small change is evaluated and refined.*

For example, in a corporate context, a company facing declining market share might not immediately launch a complete rebranding campaign, which could be risky and resource-intensive. Instead, it could implement incremental changes like improving customer service, tweaking marketing strategies, and gradually introducing new product features. This allows the company to assess the impact of each change and make further adjustments as needed, reducing the risk of large-scale failure.

Similarly, in public policy, instead of attempting to pass comprehensive legislation to address a complex issue like healthcare, policymakers might opt for smaller, targeted reforms. These could include expanding access to preventive care or implementing pilot programs for new healthcare delivery models. By "muddling through," decision-makers can navigate the complexities of their environments more effectively, making adjustments based on real-world outcomes and continuously improving their strategies.

Questions

1. *What are the key differences between intrinsic and extrinsic motivation, and how do these differences impact employee behavior and performance in the workplace?*

2.

How do motivational theories, such as Maslow's Hierarchy of Needs and Herzberg's Two-Factor Theory, apply to modern workplace settings, and what are their limitations?

3.
In what ways can managers and leaders use goal-setting theory to enhance employee motivation and performance, and what are the best practices for setting effective goals?

4.
How does an understanding of self-determination theory contribute to creating a work environment that fosters autonomy, competence, and relatedness among employees?

5.
What are some common psychological barriers to motivation, such as cognitive biases or stress, and how can managers mitigate these barriers to maintain high levels of employee motivation?

CHAPTER THREE

The Psychology of Leadership

> *"Leadership is not about being in charge. It's about taking care of those in your charge." - Simon Sinek*

Simon Sinek's quote underscores a crucial aspect of leadership psychology, emphasizing the responsibility of leaders towards their team members. It suggests that effective leadership is not merely about wielding authority or control, but rather about nurturing, supporting, and prioritizing the well-being of those under their guidance. This perspective highlights the psychological dimension of leadership, where empathy, trust, and servant leadership are essential. Leaders who prioritize the needs of their team members foster a culture of trust, collaboration, and mutual respect, ultimately leading to greater engagement, motivation, and success within the team. Effective leadership is not merely about holding a position of authority; it encompasses a complex interplay of psychological factors that shape how individuals lead, influence, and inspire others. Understanding the psychology of leadership is essential for aspiring leaders and seasoned executives alike, as it provides insights into the behaviors, traits, and motivations that drive successful leadership outcomes. This chapter sets the stage for exploring the intricate dynamics of leadership psychology. By examining the psychological underpinnings of leadership, readers will gain a deeper understanding of what it takes to lead effectively in today's dynamic and ever-evolving business landscape.

Leadership Theories

There are several leadership theories that are practical and widely applied in managerial roles.

1. *The **Contingency theory of leadership** proposes that there is no one-size-fits-all approach to leadership, and effective leadership depends on the interplay between various situational factors and leadership styles. According to this theory, different situations require different leadership styles to maximize effectiveness. For instance, in times of crisis or uncertainty, a directive or autocratic leadership style may be more appropriate for providing clear direction and guidance. In contrast, during times of stability or when dealing with highly skilled and motivated team members, a more participative or democratic leadership style may be more effective in promoting collaboration and empowerment. The Contingency theory highlights the importance of adaptability and flexibility in leadership, as leaders*

must be able to assess the demands of the situation and adjust their approach accordingly to achieve optimal outcomes.

2.

*The **Transformational theory of leadership** emphasizes the power of vision, inspiration, and personal charisma in driving organizational change and achieving extraordinary results. At its core, this theory proposes that transformational leaders inspire and motivate their followers to transcend their self-interests and work towards a higher collective purpose. These leaders possess a compelling vision for the future and have the ability to articulate it in a way that resonates with others, igniting passion and commitment among their team members. Transformational leaders also foster a culture of trust, empowerment, and innovation, encouraging followers to challenge the status quo, take risks, and pursue excellence. By empowering individuals to reach their full potential and aligning their efforts with the organization's mission and values, transformational leaders drive meaningful change and create lasting impact within their teams and organizations.*

3.

*The **Transactional leadership theory** posits that leadership is based on a transactional exchange between leaders and followers, where rewards and punishments are used to motivate and influence behavior. In this approach, leaders set clear expectations and establish performance standards, offering rewards for meeting or exceeding goals and administering corrective actions for underperformance. Transactional leaders emphasize structure, order, and compliance, relying on contingent reinforcement to maintain control and achieve organizational objectives. While transactional leadership can be effective in ensuring task completion and meeting short-term goals, it may also stifle creativity and intrinsic motivation among followers. Critics argue that transactional leadership focuses too heavily on extrinsic motivators and fails to inspire innovation or long-term engagement. Despite these limitations, transactional leadership remains a prevalent approach in many organizational contexts, particularly in settings where efficiency, consistency, and accountability are valued.*

4.

*The **Great Man theory of leadership**, rooted in the 19th-century belief in the inherent greatness of certain individuals, suggests that leadership is an innate trait possessed by a select few exceptional individuals. According to this theory, great leaders are born, not made, and possess innate qualities such as intelligence, charisma, and courage that set them apart from the average person. Proponents of this theory point to historical figures such as Abraham Lincoln, Winston Churchill, and Mahatma Gandhi as examples of great leaders who possessed these exceptional qualities and were able to inspire and lead others through times of crisis or adversity. However, critics argue that the Great Man theory oversimplifies the complexities of leadership and fails to account for the influence of situational factors, social context, and the role of followership in shaping leadership effectiveness. Despite its limitations, the Great Man theory has had a lasting impact on popular perceptions of leadership and continues to influence discussions about leadership development and succession planning.*

5.

***Behavioral leadership theory** focuses on the actions and behaviors of leaders rather than their innate traits. This theory suggests that effective leadership can be learned and developed through the adoption of specific behaviors and styles. Behavioral theorists argue that leadership effectiveness is determined by observable actions and how leaders interact with their followers and the environment. Two prominent behavioral leadership models are the Ohio State Studies and the University of Michigan Studies, which identified two key dimensions of leadership behavior: consideration (relationship-oriented) and initiating structure (task-oriented). Additionally, the Behavioral leadership theory also includes the Managerial Grid model, developed by Blake and Mouton, which evaluates leadership behavior based on a grid that considers concern for people (relationship) and concern for production (task). This theory emphasizes the importance of leadership behaviors in shaping organizational culture, motivating followers, and achieving goals. It suggests that leaders can enhance their effectiveness by adopting appropriate behaviors and adjusting their leadership style to match the needs of the situation and the preferences of their followers.*

6.

***The Leader-Member Exchange (LMX) theory**, also known as Vertical Dyad Linkage Theory, focuses on the relationships between leaders and their individual followers. According to LMX theory, leaders form unique, mutually beneficial relationships with each of their followers, rather than treating all followers the same. These relationships are characterized by varying levels of trust, support, and mutual respect, and are based on the quality of exchanges between leaders and followers. In the initial stages, leaders form "in-groups" with certain followers who demonstrate high performance, loyalty, and compatibility, while others are relegated to "out-groups." In-group members receive more attention, resources, and opportunities for advancement, while out-group members may feel marginalized or neglected. Over time, the quality of leader-member exchanges can impact job satisfaction, performance, and organizational commitment. LMX theory highlights the importance of recognizing and managing these leader-member relationships to foster a positive work environment, enhance employee engagement, and promote organizational effectiveness.*

7.

***Adaptive Leadership** is a leadership framework developed by Ronald Heifetz and his colleagues at Harvard University. Unlike traditional leadership models that focus on providing solutions and direction, adaptive leadership emphasizes the ability to navigate complex challenges and drive change in uncertain and dynamic environments. At its core, adaptive leadership involves diagnosing the root causes of problems, mobilizing stakeholders to confront difficult issues, and facilitating collective learning and adaptation. Adaptive leaders encourage experimentation, innovation, and resilience, empowering individuals and teams to tackle adaptive challenges and develop creative solutions. This approach requires leaders to be comfortable with ambiguity, tolerate dissent, and embrace failure as an opportunity for growth. By fostering a culture of adaptability and continuous improvement, adaptive leaders enable organizations to thrive in the face of change and uncertainty.*

8.

Strengths-Based Leadership *is a leadership approach that focuses on identifying and leveraging the unique strengths and talents of individuals within a team or organization. This approach emphasizes building on what individuals do best, rather than trying to fix weaknesses. Strengths-Based Leadership is rooted in positive psychology principles and suggests that individuals are more engaged, motivated, and productive when they are able to use their strengths in their work. Leaders who adopt this approach seek to understand the strengths of their team members through assessments such as the StrengthsFinder, CliftonStrengths, or VIA Character Strengths, and then align tasks, roles, and responsibilities to capitalize on those strengths. By fostering a strengths-based culture, leaders can enhance team performance, boost morale, and create a more inclusive and fulfilling work environment where individuals can thrive and reach their full potential.*

9.

Servant Leadership *is a leadership philosophy that emphasizes serving others and prioritizing the needs of followers over the leader's own interests. This approach, popularized by Robert K. Greenleaf, suggests that effective leaders are those who focus on the growth and well-being of their team members, rather than pursuing power, status, or personal gain. Servant leaders are characterized by humility, empathy, and a commitment to serving the greater good. They actively listen to their followers, empower them to contribute their best, and foster a culture of collaboration, trust, and accountability. Servant leaders are not only concerned with achieving organizational goals but also with developing the potential of individuals and promoting social justice and equity. By putting the needs of others first, servant leaders inspire loyalty, foster engagement, and create a sense of purpose and meaning within their teams and organizations.*

10.

Functional Leadership *is a leadership model that focuses on the roles and functions performed by leaders within a group or organization, rather than on specific personality traits or behaviors. This approach suggests that leadership emerges from the interaction of individuals' skills, expertise, and abilities to perform specific functions that contribute to the achievement of group goals. Functional leaders are appointed or emerge within the group based on their competence and expertise in a particular area, rather than on formal authority or hierarchical position. These leaders may fulfill various functions, such as providing technical expertise, coordinating activities, facilitating communication, or resolving conflicts, depending on the needs of the group or organization. Functional leadership emphasizes the importance of task-oriented behaviors and collaborative problem-solving in achieving collective success. By leveraging the diverse skills and capabilities of team members, functional leaders can enhance team performance, promote innovation, and drive organizational effectiveness.*

Leadership is a multifaceted concept that encompasses a diverse array of theories and approaches. From trait theories that focus on inherent characteristics to behavioral theories that emphasize observable actions, each theory offers valuable insights into the nature of leadership and how it can be effectively practiced. Whether it's through the adaptive approach of navigating change, the servant-minded ethos of serving others, or the functional model of fulfilling specific roles, leaders have a variety of tools at their disposal to inspire, motivate, and guide their teams toward success. Ultimately, effective leadership is not a one-size-fits-all proposition but rather a dynamic and evolving process that requires adaptability, empathy, and a deep understanding of the complexities of human behavior and organizational dynamics. By embracing diverse perspectives and integrating insights from various theories, leaders can cultivate the skills and strategies needed to navigate the challenges of today's rapidly changing world and drive meaningful change within their teams and organizations.

Understanding Your Leadership Style

Developing a leadership style begins with self-awareness and a deep understanding of one's own strengths, weaknesses, values, and personality traits. Effective leaders take the time to reflect on their own behavior and how it impacts others. Tools such as personality assessments, feedback from peers and subordinates, and personal reflection can provide valuable insights into one's natural leadership tendencies. For instance, some leaders may find that they naturally gravitate towards a more democratic or participative style, while others may be more comfortable with a directive or autocratic approach. By understanding their innate preferences, leaders can begin to craft a style that leverages their strengths while addressing areas for improvement.

Adapting to Different Situations

An essential aspect of developing a leadership style is the ability to adapt to different situations and the needs of the team. The Contingency theory of leadership, for example, suggests that the most effective leadership style is one that is adaptable to the specific context and challenges at hand. Leaders must be able to assess the unique demands of each situation, such as the urgency of decision-making, the complexity of the task, and the skill levels of team members. By being flexible and responsive, leaders can adjust their approach to provide the right balance of guidance, support, and autonomy, ensuring that their leadership style is effective in diverse scenarios.

Balancing Task-Oriented and People-Oriented Behaviors

Effective leadership requires a balance between task-oriented and people-oriented behaviors. Task-oriented behaviors focus on achieving goals, setting clear expectations, and ensuring that tasks are completed efficiently. People-oriented behaviors, on the other hand, prioritize building relationships, supporting team members, and fostering a positive work environment. The Behavioral leadership theory highlights the importance of both dimensions in achieving leadership effectiveness. Leaders must develop the ability to navigate this balance, understanding when to emphasize productivity and results and when to focus on the well-being and development of their team members. This balance is crucial for maintaining high performance while also ensuring team cohesion and morale.

Continuous Learning and Development

Developing a leadership style is an ongoing process that involves continuous learning and development. Leaders must remain open to new ideas, feedback, and experiences that can enhance their leadership capabilities. Engaging in professional development opportunities, such as leadership training programs, workshops, and mentoring, can provide valuable insights and skills. Additionally, leaders should cultivate a growth mindset, viewing challenges and setbacks as opportunities for learning and improvement. By committing to lifelong learning and staying attuned to the evolving needs of their team and organization, leaders can continually refine and enhance their leadership style, driving sustained success and fostering a culture of continuous improvement within their teams.

Types of Leadership Styles

- ***Autocratic Leadership****: Autocratic leadership, also known as authoritarian leadership, is characterized by individual control over all decisions with little input from team members. Managers who adopt this style make decisions unilaterally and expect subordinates to follow instructions without questioning. This style can be effective in situations requiring quick decision-making or when managing inexperienced teams needing clear guidance. However, it can also lead to low morale and creativity as team members may feel undervalued and disconnected from the decision-making process.*

- ***Democratic Leadership****: Democratic or participative leadership involves managers who actively seek input from their team members and consider their opinions in the decision-making process. This style fosters a sense of collaboration and inclusivity, which can enhance team morale, creativity, and commitment to organizational goals. While it may slow down decision-making due to the need for consensus, democratic leadership often results in more innovative solutions and increased team satisfaction, as members feel their contributions are valued and impactful.*

-

Transformational Leadership*: Transformational leadership is characterized by managers who inspire and motivate their team members to exceed their own self-interests for the sake of the organization. These leaders are visionary, charismatic, and focused on fostering a culture of continuous improvement and innovation. Transformational managers challenge the status quo and encourage their team to think creatively and take risks. This style can lead to high levels of employee engagement, motivation, and productivity, though it requires managers to be highly skilled in communication and emotional intelligence.*

- ***Transactional Leadership****: Transactional leadership is based on a system of rewards and penalties. Managers using this style set clear goals and expectations, and team members are rewarded for meeting these targets or penalized for failing to do so. This style is effective for achieving short-term tasks and maintaining routine operations. It emphasizes efficiency, structure, and control, but may not foster long-term commitment or creativity among team members as it primarily focuses on extrinsic motivation rather than intrinsic inspiration.*

- ***Laissez-Faire Leadership****: Laissez-faire leadership, or delegative leadership, is characterized by a hands-off approach where managers provide minimal direct supervision and allow team members to make decisions. This style is most effective when leading highly skilled, experienced, and self-motivated teams who require little oversight. While it can foster a strong sense of autonomy and innovation, laissez-faire leadership can also lead to a lack of direction, accountability, and consistency if team members are not adequately self-disciplined or aligned with organizational goals.*

- ***Servant Leadership****: Servant leadership focuses on prioritizing the needs of the team members and helping them grow and succeed. Managers who adopt this style lead by example, demonstrating humility, empathy, and a commitment to serving their team. This approach fosters a supportive and collaborative work environment, enhances employee well-being, and builds strong, trust-based relationships. While servant leadership can significantly boost morale and loyalty, it requires a high level of emotional intelligence and may be less effective in highly competitive or fast-paced environments where decisive action is needed.*

- ***Situational Leadership****: Situational leadership posits that there is no single best style of leadership. Instead, managers should adjust their leadership style based on the maturity, skill level, and motivation of their team members and the specifics of the task at hand. This adaptive approach ensures that the manager provides the right balance of direction and support according to the needs of the situation. Situational leadership is highly flexible and can be very effective, though it requires managers to be adept at assessing situations and versatile in their leadership capabilities.*

•

***Charismatic Leadership**: Charismatic leadership relies on the personal charm and inspirational qualities of the manager. These leaders have a magnetic personality that can inspire and energize their team. They are often seen as visionary and can create a strong emotional connection with their team members. While charismatic leadership can lead to high levels of enthusiasm and commitment, it can also result in over-reliance on the leader's presence and a potential lack of sustainable processes if the leader departs.*

By understanding and integrating various leadership styles, managers can adapt their approach to best meet the needs of their team and organizational objectives, fostering an environment of productivity, innovation, and mutual respect.

Leading by Example: Inspiring Leadership Through Action

Leadership is most powerful when it is demonstrated through action rather than words alone. Leading by example means setting the standard through personal behavior, inspiring others to follow through the power of one's deeds. This approach fosters trust, respect, and a culture of integrity within any team or organization. Many Indian leaders have embodied this principle, leaving a lasting impact through their exemplary actions.

***Mahatma Gandhi:** The Quintessential Example*

Mahatma Gandhi, one of the most iconic leaders in Indian history, epitomized leading by example. His commitment to non-violence and civil disobedience was not just a strategy but a way of life. Gandhi's famous Salt March in 1930 is a powerful example of leading by action. To protest the British monopoly on salt, Gandhi and his followers marched 240 miles to the Arabian Sea to produce salt from seawater. This act of defiance was symbolic and practical, demonstrating his commitment to challenging unjust laws through peaceful means. Gandhi's personal simplicity, his adoption of khadi (handspun cloth), and his willingness to endure hardships alongside his followers inspired millions to join the freedom struggle with the same spirit of non-violent resistance.

***APJ Abdul Kalam:** The People's President*

Dr. APJ Abdul Kalam, India's "Missile Man" and former President, is another exemplary leader who led by example. Known for his humility, dedication, and integrity, Kalam inspired millions through his life and work. As a scientist and a leader, he always emphasized the importance of hard work, innovation, and continuous learning. During his tenure as President, Kalam made it a point to meet and interact with students across the country, encouraging them to dream big and work hard to achieve their goals. His personal story of rising from a humble background to becoming a renowned scientist and the President of India serves as a beacon of hope and motivation for countless young Indians. Kalam's life demonstrated that with perseverance and integrity, one can overcome any obstacle and achieve greatness.

Ratan Tata: *Business Leadership with Compassion*

Ratan Tata, the former chairman of Tata Group, is a shining example of leading by example in the corporate world. Under his leadership, Tata Group expanded globally while adhering to high ethical standards and a strong sense of corporate social responsibility. Ratan Tata's decision to prioritize the safety and well-being of his employees and customers was evident during the 2008 Mumbai terrorist attacks. He personally visited the injured and the families of the victims, ensuring that the company provided all necessary support. His compassionate and empathetic leadership during this crisis garnered immense respect and loyalty from his employees and the public. Tata's focus on innovation, ethical business practices, and social responsibility has set a benchmark for corporate leaders in India and around the world.

Mother Teresa: *A Life of Service*

Mother Teresa, though originally from Albania, became synonymous with compassion and selfless service in India. She dedicated her life to caring for the sick, poor, and marginalized in Kolkata through the Missionaries of Charity. Mother Teresa's hands-on approach to service—personally tending to the dying and destitute—set an extraordinary example for her fellow nuns and volunteers. Her unwavering commitment to her mission, despite numerous challenges and criticisms, demonstrated the power of leading by example in the realm of humanitarian work. Her legacy continues to inspire countless individuals to engage in acts of kindness and service, reaffirming the profound impact of leadership rooted in compassion and action.

Narendra Modi: *From Humble Beginnings to National Leadership*

Narendra Modi, the current Prime Minister of India, is a prominent example of leading by example, particularly in the realm of personal discipline and hard work. Coming from a modest background and starting his career as a tea seller, Modi's journey to the highest political office in India is a testament to his dedication and perseverance. As a leader, he has consistently emphasized the importance of hard work, self-reliance, and national pride. Modi's personal habits, such as his early morning routines, strict fitness regimen, and relentless work ethic, serve as a model for his followers. His initiatives like the Swachh Bharat Abhiyan (Clean India Mission) reflect his commitment to leading by example in improving public health and sanitation, motivating millions of Indians to participate in keeping their surroundings clean.

***Kiran Bedi:** Trailblazing Woman in Law Enforcement*

Kiran Bedi, India's first female officer in the Indian Police Service (IPS), is renowned for her pioneering leadership and commitment to social justice. Throughout her career, Bedi demonstrated a fearless and innovative approach to law enforcement. One of her notable initiatives was the prison reform in Tihar Jail, where she introduced education and vocational training programs for inmates, significantly improving their rehabilitation process. Bedi's hands-on involvement and her strict yet compassionate leadership style earned her immense respect and set a powerful example for future generations of law enforcement officers. Her personal integrity and dedication to public service continue to inspire women and men across India to pursue careers in policing and public administration.

***Narayana Murthy:** Ethical Leadership in Business*

Narayana Murthy, the co-founder of Infosys, is celebrated for his ethical leadership and commitment to corporate governance. Under his leadership, Infosys became one of India's most respected and successful IT companies, known for its transparency, innovation, and employee-friendly policies. Murthy led by example by maintaining high ethical standards and fostering a culture of meritocracy and fairness within the company. His decision to implement transparent financial practices and share wealth creation with employees through stock options set new benchmarks in the Indian corporate sector. Murthy's leadership style, characterized by humility, integrity, and a focus on social responsibility, has inspired countless entrepreneurs and business leaders in India and beyond.

***Sunder Pichai:** Humble Leadership in Global Tech*

Sundar Pichai, the CEO of Alphabet Inc. and its subsidiary Google LLC, exemplifies the power of leading by example in the global tech industry. Pichai's journey from a modest upbringing in Chennai to leading one of the world's most influential technology companies is a story of hard work, innovation, and empathetic leadership. Known for his calm demeanor and collaborative approach, Pichai has consistently emphasized the importancc of humility, continuous learning, and inclusivity. His leadership during times of significant challenges, such as navigating regulatory scrutiny and addressing ethical concerns within the tech industry, has been marked by transparency and a commitment to upholding Google's core values. Pichai's personal journey and leadership style serve as an inspiration to aspiring tech professionals and leaders worldwide.

***Ela Bhatt**: Pioneer of Women's Empowerment*

Ela Bhatt, the founder of the Self-Employed Women's Association (SEWA), has made remarkable contributions to the empowerment of women in India, particularly those working in the informal sector. SEWA, a trade union for poor, self-employed women workers, provides them with support in areas such as finance, healthcare, and legal rights. Bhatt's advocacy for the economic and social rights of women has led to improved livelihoods and greater recognition of women's contributions to the economy. Her efforts have inspired similar movements globally, advocating for the dignity and rights of informal workers.

***Verghese Kurien**: Father of the White Revolution*

Verghese Kurien, the architect of India's White Revolution, transformed the country from a milk-deficient nation into the world's largest milk producer. His leadership in establishing the cooperative dairy movement, particularly through the creation of the Amul brand, revolutionized the dairy industry and uplifted millions of rural farmers. Kurien's innovative approach to dairy farming and cooperative management empowered farmers with better income and ensured a reliable supply of milk to urban areas. His work significantly contributed to improving nutrition and rural development in India.

These stories of Indian leaders highlight the profound impact of leading by example. By embodying the values they espouse and demonstrating commitment through their actions, these leaders have inspired generations and created lasting change. Their legacies serve as powerful reminders that true leadership is not about commanding from above but about guiding and inspiring through lived example.

***Dr. B.R. Ambedkar**: Architect of the Indian Constitution*

Dr. Bhimrao Ramji Ambedkar, commonly known as Babasaheb Ambedkar, played a pivotal role in shaping modern India through his tireless advocacy for social justice and equality. As the principal architect of the Indian Constitution, Ambedkar laid the foundation for a democratic and inclusive society. He championed the rights of marginalized communities, particularly the Dalits, and worked to eradicate social discrimination and untouchability. Ambedkar's contributions extend beyond the legal framework; he was also a renowned economist, social reformer, and politician who dedicated his life to improving the lives of the underprivileged and promoting social harmony.

***Kailash Satyarthi**: Crusader Against Child Labor*

Kailash Satyarthi is a renowned child rights activist who has dedicated his life to the eradication of child labor and the promotion of children's education. As the founder of Bachpan Bachao Andolan (Save Childhood Movement), Satyarthi has rescued tens of thousands of children from forced labor, trafficking, and slavery. His relentless efforts have brought international attention to the plight of child laborers and have led to significant policy changes in India and abroad. In recognition of his tireless work, Satyarthi was awarded the Nobel Peace Prize in 2014, alongside Malala Yousafzai. His advocacy continues to inspire global action towards ensuring every child's right to a safe and healthy childhood, free from exploitation and abuse.

Questions:

1. *Compare and contrast transformational leadership and transactional leadership. How do these leadership styles impact employee motivation and organizational performance?*

2. *What are the key characteristics of servant leadership, and how does this leadership style influence organizational culture and employee satisfaction?*

3. *Discuss the main principles of the situational leadership theory developed by Hersey and Blanchard. How can leaders effectively adapt their style according to the readiness level of their followers?*

4. *Explain the concept of charismatic leadership. What are the potential advantages and disadvantages of relying on a charismatic leader within an organization?*

5. *How does the path-goal theory of leadership propose that leaders can enhance employee performance and satisfaction? Provide examples of different leadership behaviors outlined in this theory.*

CHAPTER FOUR

Emotion in the Workplace

> *"Emotions in the workplace are like an uninvited guest – you can ignore them, but they won't go away."*

This quote highlights the inevitability and persistence of emotions in the workplace. It underscores the importance of acknowledging and managing emotions rather than ignoring them, as they play a significant role in overall workplace dynamics, productivity, and employee well-being. Emotions play a critical role in the workplace, influencing everything from individual performance and team dynamics to organizational culture and leadership effectiveness. Unlike the outdated notion that emotions should be left at the door when entering the office, modern research and practice recognize that emotions are integral to how we work and interact with others. Understanding and managing emotions can lead to better decision-making, enhanced creativity, and improved overall well-being at work.

- ***The Impact of Positive Emotions***

Positive emotions, such as joy, enthusiasm, and pride, can significantly enhance workplace outcomes. They foster a more collaborative and innovative environment, improve job satisfaction, and boost productivity. For instance, consider the case of a tech startup where the founder, Lisa, cultivates a culture of positivity and support. During team meetings, she encourages open sharing of successes and celebrates small victories. This approach not only motivates employees but also creates a sense of belonging and community. As a result, the team feels more engaged and invested in their work, leading to higher levels of creativity and innovation.

- ***The Challenge of Negative Emotions***

While positive emotions can enhance workplace dynamics, negative emotions such as stress, frustration, and anger can have detrimental effects if not managed properly. Negative emotions can lead to conflicts, reduced productivity, and higher turnover rates. For example, in a high-pressure sales environment, an employee named Tom feels overwhelmed by unrealistic targets and tight deadlines. His frustration leads to frequent conflicts with colleagues and a decline in his performance. Recognizing the impact of negative emotions, Tom's manager intervenes by providing additional support, adjusting his workload, and encouraging open communication. These actions help mitigate Tom's stress and improve his emotional state, ultimately enhancing his performance and relationships at work.

- ### *Emotional Intelligence and Leadership*

Emotional intelligence (EI) is the ability to understand and manage one's own emotions, as well as the emotions of others. High EI is a crucial trait for effective leadership. Leaders with high emotional intelligence can navigate complex interpersonal dynamics, inspire and motivate their teams, and create a positive work environment. For instance, Sarah, a project manager at a marketing firm, excels in emotional intelligence. When her team faces a major setback with a client project, she remains calm and empathetic. She acknowledges the team's disappointment, encourages them to express their concerns, and works collaboratively to find solutions. Sarah's ability to manage her own emotions and support her team helps them recover quickly and stay focused on their goals.

- ### *Research Insights on Emotion in the Workplace*

Research supports the significant role of emotions in the workplace. Studies have shown that positive emotions can enhance cognitive functioning, improve problem-solving abilities, and increase resilience to stress. Conversely, unmanaged negative emotions can lead to burnout, absenteeism, and decreased job performance. Organizations that prioritize emotional well-being through supportive policies, employee assistance programs, and training in emotional intelligence tend to have more engaged and productive workforces.

- ### *Embracing Emotion in the Workplace*

Embracing emotions in the workplace is not just about creating a happier environment—it's about leveraging the full spectrum of human experience to drive better outcomes. By understanding and managing emotions, both positive and negative, organizations can create a more dynamic, innovative, and resilient workforce. As the example of Lisa's tech startup and Sarah's marketing team illustrate, recognizing and addressing emotions can lead to enhanced collaboration, creativity, and overall success in the workplace.

Emotional Intelligence

Emotional Intelligence (EI), often referred to as Emotional Quotient (EQ), is the ability to recognize, understand, manage, and influence one's own emotions and the emotions of others. First popularized by psychologist Daniel Goleman, EI is a critical skill that contributes to effective leadership, enhanced interpersonal relationships, and overall workplace success. Unlike traditional measures of intelligence, such as IQ, which focus on cognitive abilities, EI encompasses a range of skills related to emotional awareness and regulation.

Core Components of Emotional Intelligence

Goleman identified five key components of emotional intelligence:

1. ***Self-Awareness:*** *The ability to recognize and understand one's own emotions. Self-aware individuals are conscious of their emotional states, what triggers them, and how their emotions impact their thoughts and behaviors. For example, a self-aware manager might notice feelings of frustration rising during a tense meeting and choose to pause and breathe deeply before responding, rather than reacting impulsively.*

2. ***Self-Regulation:*** *The ability to manage and control one's emotions in healthy ways. This involves staying calm under pressure, managing stress, and avoiding hasty decisions driven by negative emotions. A practical example is an employee who receives critical feedback and, instead of reacting defensively, takes time to reflect on the feedback and uses it constructively to improve performance.*

3. ***Motivation:*** *The ability to harness emotions to pursue goals with energy and persistence. Motivated individuals are driven by an intrinsic desire to achieve and are often more resilient and optimistic. For instance, a motivated salesperson who faces a series of rejections might use the setbacks as motivation to refine their approach and work harder to secure new clients.*

4.

Empathy: *The ability to understand and share the feelings of others. Empathy involves recognizing emotional cues and responding appropriately, which is essential for building strong relationships and effective communication. For example, a team leader who notices a team member is unusually quiet and withdrawn might check in privately to offer support, showing empathy and concern.*

5\. ***Social Skills:*** *The ability to manage relationships and build networks. This includes skills such as effective communication, conflict resolution, and collaboration. A leader with strong social skills can navigate complex social situations, build rapport with colleagues, and foster a cooperative team environment.*

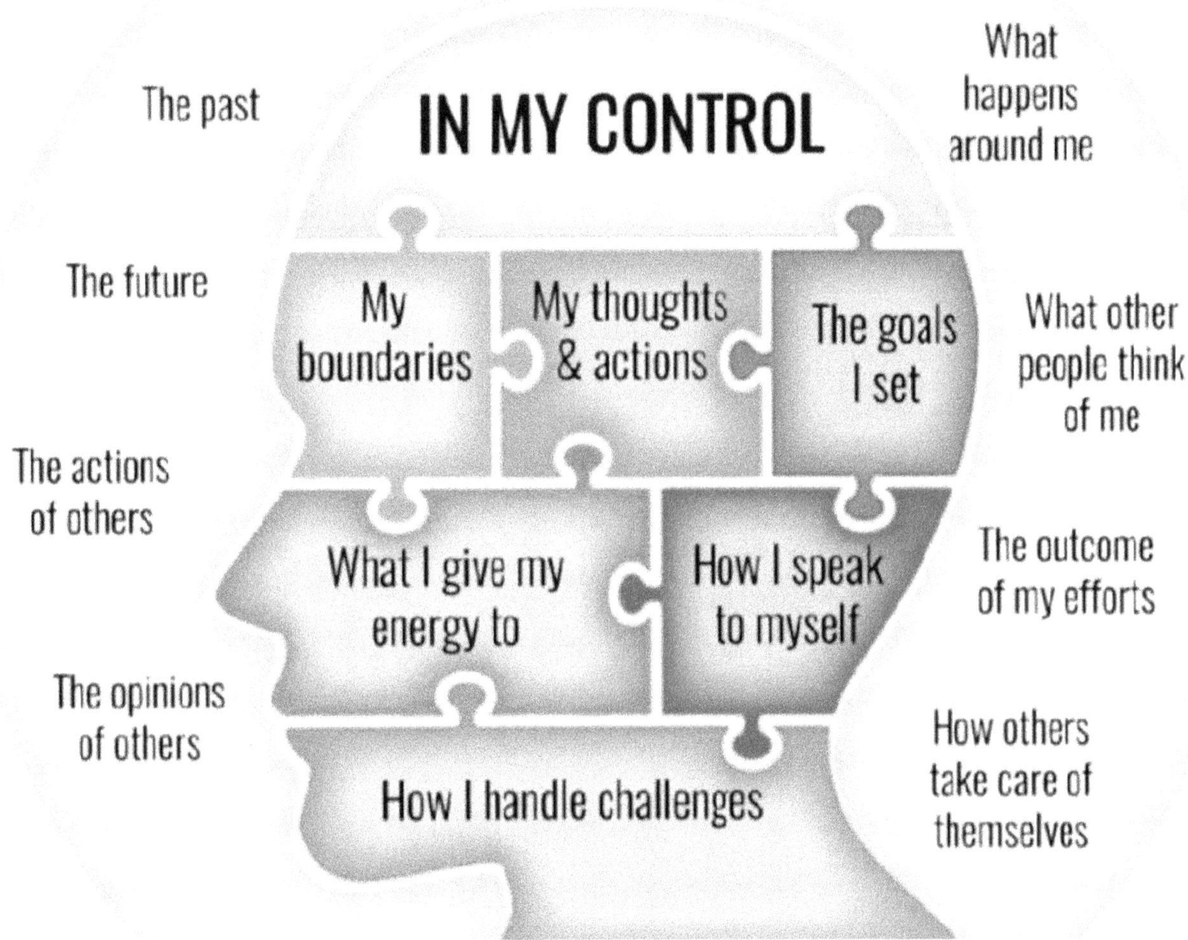

Emotional Intelligence

The Importance of Emotional Intelligence in the Workplace

Emotional intelligence is crucial in the workplace for several reasons:

Enhanced Leadership: Leaders with high EI can inspire and motivate their teams, manage stress effectively, and create a positive work environment. They are adept at navigating interpersonal conflicts and fostering a culture of collaboration and trust. For example, a leader who demonstrates empathy and actively listens to their employees can build a more loyal and engaged team.

Improved Team Dynamics: Teams with emotionally intelligent members tend to have better communication, reduced conflict, and higher levels of cooperation. Emotional intelligence helps team members understand each other's perspectives and work together more harmoniously. In a diverse team, EI can bridge cultural and personal differences, leading to more inclusive and effective teamwork.

Better Decision-Making: Emotions play a significant role in decision-making. Individuals with high EI can manage their emotions and remain objective, leading to more balanced and rational decisions. For instance, a manager who can control their anxiety during a crisis can make clearer, more strategic decisions.

Increased Job Performance: Employees with high EI are often more adaptable, resilient, and capable of handling stress. They can navigate the complexities of the workplace more effectively, leading to better job performance and career advancement. An emotionally intelligent employee who handles criticism well and remains motivated can continuously improve and excel in their role.

Examples of Emotional Intelligence in Action

Case Study: Leadership in Crisis: During a major corporate merger, tensions were high at a manufacturing company. Employees were anxious about job security and changes in the organizational structure. The CEO, known for his high emotional intelligence, held a series of town hall meetings to address concerns. He listened actively, acknowledged the employees' fears, and communicated transparently about the steps being taken to ensure a smooth transition. By showing empathy and providing clear information, he alleviated much of the anxiety and maintained morale throughout the process.

Case Study: Conflict Resolution: In a tech startup, two key team members were in constant conflict, which was affecting the whole team's performance. The project manager, who had strong social skills, decided to intervene. She facilitated a mediation session where each party could express their concerns and feelings openly. By acknowledging their emotions and helping them understand each other's perspectives, she managed to resolve the conflict and restore a productive working relationship.

Case Study: Sales Motivation: A sales manager noticed that her team was feeling demotivated after a series of failed pitches. She decided to boost morale by recognizing small wins and setting achievable short-term goals to rebuild their confidence. Additionally, she held regular one-on-one meetings to understand their individual challenges and provided personalized support and encouragement. Her approach not only improved the team's performance but also strengthened their commitment to the organization.

Research Insights on Emotional Intelligence

Research supports the significant impact of emotional intelligence on various aspects of professional and personal life:

Performance and Leadership: Studies have shown that leaders with high emotional intelligence tend to have more satisfied and productive teams. Their ability to manage emotions and build strong relationships translates into better leadership outcomes.

Stress and Well-Being: Emotional intelligence is linked to lower stress levels and better mental health. Individuals with high EI can manage stress more effectively, leading to improved well-being and job satisfaction.

Conflict Management: Research indicates that emotional intelligence is crucial for conflict resolution. People with high EI are better at navigating conflicts and finding mutually beneficial solutions, which is essential for maintaining a positive work environment.

Cultivating Emotional Intelligence

Emotional intelligence is a vital skill that can be developed and enhanced over time. Organizations can benefit from training programs that focus on building self-awareness, self-regulation, motivation, empathy, and social skills. By fostering emotional intelligence, companies can create a more supportive, collaborative, and productive workplace, where employees thrive both professionally and personally. Whether navigating everyday challenges or leading through change, emotional intelligence equips individuals and leaders with the tools to succeed and foster positive relationships within the organization.

Managing Stress and Emotions

Stress and emotions are integral aspects of the workplace, impacting employee performance, job satisfaction, and overall organizational health. Effectively managing stress and emotions is crucial for maintaining a productive and positive work environment. While stress is an inevitable part of professional life, understanding its sources, effects, and management strategies can help individuals and organizations thrive. Emotion management is equally important, as it influences decision-making, interpersonal relationships, and mental well-being.

Understanding Stress in the Workplace

Stress is the body's response to perceived challenges or threats. It can be triggered by various factors, including workload, deadlines, interpersonal conflicts, and organizational changes. While a certain level of stress can be motivating, chronic stress can lead to burnout, decreased productivity, and health issues. Recognizing the signs of stress and its sources is the first step in managing it effectively.

Sources of Workplace Stress

- *Workload and Time Pressure: Excessive workload and tight deadlines are common sources of stress. Employees may feel overwhelmed by the volume of tasks and the need to meet high expectations within limited time frames.*
- *Interpersonal Relationships: Conflicts with colleagues, supervisors, or clients can create a stressful work environment. Poor communication, lack of support, and workplace bullying are significant stressors.*
- *Organizational Changes: Changes such as mergers, restructuring, or new technology implementations can disrupt routines and create uncertainty, leading to stress.*
- *Work-Life Balance: Difficulty in balancing professional and personal responsibilities can result in stress. Long working hours and lack of flexibility contribute to this issue.*
- *Job Security: Concerns about job stability, especially in volatile economic conditions, can be a major source of stress for employees.*
- *Effects of Stress on Employees and Organizations*

- *Chronic stress can have wide-ranging effects on both employees and organizations:*

- *Health Issues: Prolonged stress can lead to physical health problems such as hypertension, cardiovascular diseases, and weakened immune systems. It also contributes to mental health issues like anxiety and depression.*

- *Decreased Productivity: Stress impairs cognitive functions such as concentration, decision-making, and memory, leading to reduced productivity and errors.*

- *Increased Absenteeism: High stress levels can result in increased absenteeism as employees take time off to recover from stress-related health problems.*

- *Low Morale and Engagement: Persistent stress can lead to low morale, decreased job satisfaction, and disengagement from work, affecting overall organizational performance.*

- *High Turnover: Stressful work environments can lead to higher employee turnover rates, increasing recruitment and training costs for organizations.*

Strategies for Managing Stress

Effective stress management involves a combination of individual and organizational strategies:

Individual Strategies:

- *Time Management: Prioritizing tasks, setting realistic goals, and breaking tasks into manageable chunks can help reduce workload-related stress.*

- *Healthy Lifestyle: Regular exercise, a balanced diet, and adequate sleep are essential for managing stress. Physical activity releases endorphins, which improve mood and reduce stress.*

- *Mindfulness and Relaxation Techniques: Practices such as meditation, deep breathing exercises, and yoga can help individuals manage stress by promoting relaxation and emotional balance.*

- *Seeking Support: Talking to friends, family, or mental health professionals can provide emotional support and practical advice for managing stress.*

Organizational Strategies:

- *Supportive Work Environment: Creating a supportive and inclusive work culture where employees feel valued and heard can significantly reduce stress.*
- *Workload Management: Ensuring reasonable workloads and providing resources to manage tasks effectively can help alleviate stress.*
- *Flexible Work Arrangements: Offering flexible working hours, remote work options, and opportunities for work-life balance can reduce stress.*
- *Employee Assistance Programs: Providing access to counseling services, stress management workshops, and wellness programs can support employees in managing stress.*

Examples of Effective Stress Management

Case Study: *Tech Company Implements Wellness Program: A leading tech company recognized the high stress levels among its employees due to demanding project deadlines. To address this, the company introduced a comprehensive wellness program that included on-site fitness classes, meditation sessions, and access to mental health counselors. The program also offered flexible working hours and remote work options. As a result, employees reported lower stress levels, improved job satisfaction, and increased productivity.*

Case Study: *Retail Chain Enhances Work-Life Balance: A large retail chain observed high turnover rates and low morale among its employees. To improve the situation, the company implemented policies that promoted work-life balance, such as flexible scheduling, part-time work options, and paid time off for personal and family needs. These changes led to a significant decrease in turnover rates and higher employee engagement.*

Emotion Management in the Workplace

Managing emotions is crucial for maintaining a healthy and productive work environment. Emotions influence how employees interact with each other, handle stress, and perform their tasks. Emotion management involves recognizing, understanding, and regulating emotions to ensure they positively impact workplace interactions and outcomes.

Strategies for Managing Emotions

Emotional Awareness: Being aware of one's emotions and their impact on behavior is the first step in managing them. Self-awareness helps individuals recognize emotional triggers and respond appropriately.

Emotional Regulation: Techniques such as deep breathing, positive self-talk, and mindfulness can help individuals manage intense emotions and maintain emotional balance.

Empathy and Social Skills: Developing empathy and effective communication skills can enhance interpersonal relationships and reduce conflicts. Understanding and addressing the emotions of others fosters a supportive work environment.

Constructive Expression: Encouraging employees to express their emotions constructively through open communication channels, feedback sessions, and team-building activities can improve emotional well-being.

Examples of Emotion Management

***Case Study:** Manager Uses Emotional Intelligence to Navigate Team Conflict: At a marketing firm, a team experienced tension due to differing opinions on a project. The manager, who had high emotional intelligence, facilitated a meeting where team members could express their concerns and feelings openly. By listening actively and showing empathy, the manager helped the team understand each other's perspectives and work towards a collaborative solution. This approach not only resolved the conflict but also strengthened team cohesion.*

Case Study: *Employee Overcomes Anxiety with Supportive Leadership: In a finance company, an employee named Jane often felt anxious during high-stakes presentations. Her manager noticed this and offered to help her practice and prepare. The manager provided constructive feedback and encouraged Jane to use relaxation techniques before presentations. With this support, Jane's confidence grew, and her anxiety decreased, leading to better performance and greater job satisfaction.*

Research Insights on Stress and Emotion Management

- *Impact on Performance: Studies show that well-managed stress and emotions lead to higher job performance, increased creativity, and better problem-solving abilities.*
- *Health and Well-Being: Effective stress management is linked to improved physical and mental health, reducing the risk of burnout and other stress-related conditions.*
- *Organizational Benefits: Organizations that prioritize stress and emotion management tend to have lower turnover rates, higher employee engagement, and better overall performance.*

Fostering a Supportive Work Environment

Managing stress and emotions is essential for creating a healthy, productive, and positive work environment. By implementing individual and organizational strategies to address stress and support emotional well-being, organizations can enhance employee satisfaction, performance, and retention. As illustrated by the examples of the tech company and the retail chain, proactive measures to manage stress and emotions can lead to significant improvements in workplace dynamics and overall success. Recognizing the integral role of stress and emotions in the workplace and addressing them effectively is key to fostering a thriving organizational culture.

The Role of Emotions in Leadership

Emotions are a powerful force in leadership, shaping how leaders perceive situations, make decisions, and interact with their teams. Effective leadership is not solely about strategic vision or technical skills; it also involves emotional intelligence—the ability to understand and manage one's own emotions and the emotions of others. Leaders who harness the power of emotions can inspire, motivate, and connect with their teams on a deeper level, driving better organizational outcomes.

The Impact of Emotions on Leadership Effectiveness

Emotional intelligence in leadership encompasses several key components: self-awareness, self-regulation, motivation, empathy, and social skills. Each of these elements plays a crucial role in how leaders manage their emotions and influence their teams.

- *Self-Awareness: Leaders who are self-aware understand their emotional triggers and how their feelings affect their behavior and decision-making. For example, a self-aware leader might recognize that they become impatient during high-pressure situations and take steps to remain calm and composed, ensuring their actions are deliberate and constructive.*
- *Self-Regulation: Effective leaders can control their emotions and respond to challenges with a balanced and thoughtful approach. A leader who can manage their frustration during a setback will be better equipped to maintain a positive environment and motivate their team to persevere.*
- *Motivation: Emotionally intelligent leaders are driven by intrinsic motivation and a passion for their work. They can maintain a positive attitude and inspire others, even in the face of difficulties. For instance, a motivated leader might use a vision of the team's success to keep everyone focused and energized during a challenging project.*
- *Empathy: Understanding and sharing the feelings of others is a critical skill for leaders. Empathy allows leaders to connect with their team members, understand their needs and concerns, and provide appropriate support. A leader who shows empathy during times of personal or professional stress can build trust and loyalty within their team.*
- *Social Skills: Strong social skills enable leaders to communicate effectively, resolve conflicts, and foster a collaborative team environment. Leaders with these skills can navigate complex social dynamics and build strong, cohesive teams.*

Examples of Emotional Intelligence in Leadership

Case Study: *Transformational Leadership in a Healthcare Setting: Dr. Smith, the head of a hospital department, faced a crisis when her team was overwhelmed by an influx of patients.*

Instead of reacting with panic, Dr. Smith remained calm and supportive. She actively listened to her team's concerns, provided reassurance, and worked collaboratively to find solutions. Her empathetic and composed approach helped the team navigate the crisis effectively, maintaining high levels of care and morale.

Case Study: *Empathy in Corporate Leadership: During a period of downsizing at a financial firm, the CEO, John, held multiple meetings with affected employees. He listened to their concerns, provided transparent information about the reasons for the downsizing, and offered support through outplacement services. John's empathetic handling of the situation helped maintain trust and respect among remaining employees, preserving the firm's morale and reputation.*

Research Insights on Emotions in Leadership

- *Performance and Decision-Making: Studies indicate that leaders with high emotional intelligence make better decisions, particularly in high-stress situations. Their ability to remain calm and objective helps them assess situations accurately and choose the best course of action.*
- *Employee Engagement and Retention: Emotionally intelligent leaders are more likely to foster positive relationships with their employees, leading to higher engagement and lower turnover rates. Employees feel valued and understood, which enhances their commitment to the organization.*
- *Organizational Climate and Culture: Leaders who manage their emotions well contribute to a positive organizational climate. Their behavior sets the tone for the workplace, influencing the overall culture and employee satisfaction.*

Strategies for Developing Emotional Intelligence in Leadership

Self-Reflection and Feedback: Leaders can improve their emotional intelligence through regular self-reflection and seeking feedback from peers and subordinates. Understanding their strengths and areas for improvement helps leaders develop greater self-awareness and self-regulation.

- *Training and Development: Organizations can offer training programs focused on emotional intelligence, including workshops on empathy, communication skills, and stress management. These programs equip leaders with the tools they need to enhance their emotional intelligence.*

- *Mindfulness Practices: Techniques such as mindfulness meditation can help leaders stay present and manage their emotions effectively. Mindfulness practices improve self-awareness and emotional regulation, enabling leaders to respond thoughtfully rather than react impulsively.*

- *Mentorship and Coaching: Mentoring and coaching relationships provide leaders with guidance and support in developing their emotional intelligence. Experienced mentors can share insights and strategies for managing emotions and navigating complex interpersonal dynamics.*

Embracing Emotions in Leadership

Emotional intelligence is a critical component of effective leadership. By understanding and managing their own emotions and those of their team members, leaders can create a positive, motivating, and productive work environment. The examples of Dr. Smith and John demonstrate how emotionally intelligent leadership can inspire trust, foster resilience, and drive organizational success. As research and practical experience show, leaders who embrace and harness the power of emotions are better equipped to lead their teams through challenges and achieve lasting success. Organizations that prioritize the development of emotional intelligence in their leaders will benefit from improved decision-making, enhanced employee engagement, and a stronger organizational culture.

Questions:

1. *How does emotional intelligence (EI) contribute to effective leadership and team dynamics in the workplace? Provide examples of how high EI can improve workplace relationships.*

2. *What are the primary sources of stress in the workplace, and how can organizations implement strategies to reduce employee stress and enhance well-being?*

3. *Discuss the impact of workplace emotions on job performance and decision-making. How can managers recognize and address negative emotions to maintain a productive work environment?*

4.

Explain the role of emotional regulation in managing stress at work. What techniques can employees use to better regulate their emotions during high-pressure situations?

5.

How can organizations foster a culture that promotes emotional intelligence and supports employees in managing their stress? What specific training or initiatives can be implemented to achieve this goal?

CHAPTER FIVE

Perception and Decision Making

"We see the world not as it is, but as we are." — Anaïs Nin

This quote by Anaïs Nin highlights the subjective nature of perception and its impact on decision-making. It underscores the idea that our personal experiences, biases, and emotions shape how we interpret the world around us, influencing the decisions we make. Perception and decision-making are fundamental psychological processes that shape how we interpret the world around us and make choices in our personal and professional lives. Perception involves the way we see, hear, and understand information from our environment. It's like putting together a puzzle, where our brain pieces together various sensory inputs to form a coherent picture. For instance, consider a manager walking into a noisy office. She might perceive the buzz of conversations and the sight of busy employees as signs of productivity and engagement. However, another manager might see the same scene and perceive it as chaotic and disorganized. This example highlights how perception can vary from person to person based on past experiences, expectations, and individual biases.

Decision-making, on the other hand, is the process of choosing between different options or courses of action. It's a bit like being at a crossroads and having to decide which path to take. Research shows that our decisions are heavily influenced by how we perceive situations. For example, a company deciding whether to launch a new product might rely on market research and customer feedback. If the perception of potential success is high, they are more likely to go ahead with the launch. However, if past experiences of failed products cloud their perception, they might decide against it. This intertwining of perception and decision-making illustrates the complexity of these processes.

Studies have shown that perception and decision-making are not always rational. Cognitive biases, such as confirmation bias, where people favor information that confirms their preconceptions, can skew both perception and decision-making. For instance, if a leader believes that a particular employee is highly competent, they might perceive the employee's actions in a more favorable light, overlooking mistakes. This can lead to biased decision-making regarding promotions or assignments. Research in psychology and behavioral economics has uncovered numerous such biases, highlighting that our perceptions and decisions are often influenced by subconscious factors rather than purely logical reasoning.

By understanding how perception and decision-making work, managers can make more informed and fair decisions, recognize their own biases, and create an environment where diverse perspectives are valued. In the following sections, we will explore these concepts in more detail, providing insights and strategies for improving managerial practices.

How Managers Perceive Situations in an Organization

- #### *Role of Experience and Expertise*

Managers' perceptions of organizational situations are significantly shaped by their experience and expertise. Experienced managers often rely on their past encounters to interpret current events, drawing parallels and using prior knowledge to assess situations quickly. For instance, a manager who has successfully navigated a financial downturn in the past may perceive current budget cuts as manageable challenges rather than insurmountable obstacles. Expertise in a specific area, such as marketing or operations, also influences perception. A marketing manager might focus on customer sentiment and brand impact when evaluating a new product launch, while an operations manager might prioritize production efficiency and logistics.

- #### *Impact of Cognitive Biases*

Cognitive biases are another crucial factor influencing managerial perception. These biases are mental shortcuts that can distort a manager's interpretation of situations. For example, confirmation bias may lead a manager to favor information that supports their existing beliefs while disregarding contradictory data. A manager confident in their team's abilities might overlook early warning signs of project delays due to overconfidence bias. Recognizing and mitigating these biases is essential for managers to perceive situations more accurately and make better-informed decisions.

- ***Influence of Organizational Culture***

The organizational culture within which managers operate also plays a vital role in shaping their perceptions. A culture that values innovation and risk-taking can lead managers to perceive new ideas and unconventional approaches more positively. Conversely, in a risk-averse culture, managers might view the same ideas as too risky and prefer to stick with traditional methods. Additionally, a collaborative culture encourages managers to seek input from diverse perspectives, enriching their understanding and perception of complex situations.

- ***External and Internal Environmental Factors***

External and internal environmental factors further affect how managers perceive situations. External factors include market trends, economic conditions, and competitive pressures. For instance, a manager might perceive a dip in sales as a result of broader economic downturns rather than internal failings. Internal factors encompass organizational dynamics such as employee morale, interdepartmental relationships, and internal processes. A manager aware of low employee morale might interpret increased absenteeism as a sign of deeper organizational issues rather than individual disengagement.

- ***Emotional State and Stress Levels***

A manager's emotional state and stress levels can also cloud their perception. High stress can narrow a manager's focus, making them more likely to perceive situations as crises. For instance, a manager under significant pressure might see a minor setback as a major issue, leading to overreaction. Conversely, a manager in a positive emotional state may have a more optimistic view, potentially underestimating risks. Balancing emotional awareness and stress management is crucial for maintaining clear and objective perception.

- ***Integration of Diverse Inputs***

Finally, effective managers integrate diverse inputs to form a comprehensive perception of organizational situations. This involves actively seeking feedback from team members, consulting with other departments, and considering both quantitative data and qualitative insights. For example, when assessing the potential success of a new initiative, a manager might combine market research data with insights from customer service teams and anecdotal feedback from sales representatives. This holistic approach ensures a well-rounded perception, facilitating more balanced and informed decision-making.

By understanding these factors and actively working to mitigate biases and integrate diverse perspectives, managers can enhance their perception of situations within the organization. This improved perception leads to better strategic planning, problem-solving, and overall decision-making, contributing to organizational success.

How to Have Clear Perception and Make the Right Decision

Having a clear perception and making the right decisions are crucial skills in both personal and professional contexts. Here are some strategies to help you achieve clarity in perception and improve decision-making:

1. Self-Awareness and Mindfulness

Practice Self-Reflection: Regularly take time to reflect on your thoughts, feelings, and biases. Understanding your own mental filters can help you recognize when they might be distorting your perception.

Mindfulness Meditation: Engage in mindfulness practices to stay present and reduce the influence of stress or anxiety on your perception. Mindfulness helps in maintaining a clear, focused mind.

2. Seek Diverse Perspectives

Consult with Others: Before making important decisions, seek input from a diverse group of people. Different perspectives can provide new insights and help counteract your own biases.

Encourage Open Dialogue: Foster an environment where team members feel comfortable sharing their viewpoints and challenging assumptions. This can lead to more well-rounded and informed decisions.

3. Gather Comprehensive Information

Research Thoroughly: Base your decisions on comprehensive data and reliable sources. Avoid relying solely on first impressions or incomplete information.

Verify Facts: Cross-check information from multiple sources to ensure accuracy and avoid being misled by false or biased data.

4. Recognize and Mitigate Biases

Identify Common Biases: Be aware of common cognitive biases, such as confirmation bias, availability heuristic, and anchoring. Recognizing these biases can help you take steps to mitigate their impact.

Use Decision-Making Frameworks: Employ structured decision-making frameworks, such as SWOT analysis (Strengths, Weaknesses, Opportunities, Threats) or the DECIDE model (Define, Establish criteria, Consider alternatives, Identify best alternative, Develop plan, Evaluate), to minimize the influence of biases.

5. Embrace Critical Thinking

Question Assumptions: Regularly challenge your assumptions and consider alternative explanations. Critical thinking involves analyzing information objectively and systematically.

Evaluate Pros and Cons: Weigh the potential benefits and drawbacks of each option. This can help you make more balanced and rational decisions.

6. Learn from Past Experiences

Reflect on Previous Decisions: Analyze past decisions to understand what worked well and what didn't. Learning from successes and failures can improve future decision-making.

Seek Feedback: After making decisions, seek feedback on their outcomes. Constructive feedback can provide valuable lessons and insights for future decisions.

7. Stay Flexible and Open to Change

Adaptability: Be prepared to adapt your perceptions and decisions as new information becomes available. Flexibility allows you to respond effectively to changing circumstances.

Continuous Learning: Stay informed about new research, trends, and best practices in your field. Continuous learning helps keep your perception sharp and your decision-making skills up to date.

By applying these strategies, you can develop clearer perceptions and make more informed, rational decisions. Whether you're managing a team, leading a project, or navigating personal choices, these skills will enhance your ability to achieve successful outcomes and drive positive results.

Attribution Theory

Attribution theory, developed by Fritz Heider and further expanded by Harold Kelley and Bernard Weiner, examines how individuals interpret and assign causes to events and behaviors. The theory suggests that people tend to attribute others' actions either to internal factors (such as personality traits, motives, or intentions) or external factors (such as situational pressures or environmental influences). For example, if an employee misses a deadline, a manager might attribute this behavior to the employee's lack of effort (an internal attribution) or to unforeseen challenges in the project (an external attribution). The way these attributions are made significantly affects how we understand and respond to others' behaviors.

Attribution theory also highlights common biases that influence our attributions. One such bias is the fundamental attribution error, where individuals overemphasize internal factors and underestimate external factors when explaining others' behaviors. For instance, a manager might blame an employee's poor performance on laziness rather than considering external factors like insufficient training or unrealistic workload. Conversely, the self-serving bias leads people to attribute their successes to internal factors (such as skill or effort) and their failures to external factors (such as bad luck or difficult circumstances). Understanding these biases can help individuals make more accurate attributions and foster better interpersonal relationships.

Perception and decision-making are intricately linked through the lens of attribution theory. How we perceive and attribute causes to behaviors directly influences the decisions we make regarding others. For instance, a manager's perception of an employee's missed deadline as a result of laziness (an internal attribution) might lead to a decision to reprimand the employee. In contrast, perceiving the same behavior due to external factors, like a sudden increase in workload, might lead to a decision to provide additional support or resources. Thus, the initial perception shapes the subsequent decision-making process. By being aware of attribution biases and striving for a balanced view, managers and leaders can make more fair and effective decisions, ultimately improving organizational outcomes and fostering a positive work environment.

Individual Differences and Decision Making

Individual differences significantly influence how decisions are made within organizations. These differences can include a wide range of factors such as personality traits, cognitive styles, emotional intelligence, experience, and values. For example, a risk-averse person may make more conservative decisions, preferring safer, more predictable outcomes. In contrast, a risk-taker might opt for bold and innovative solutions, even if they carry higher risks. Cognitive styles, such as analytical versus intuitive thinking, also play a role. An analytical thinker might rely on detailed data and systematic processes to make decisions, while an intuitive thinker may base decisions on gut feelings and experiences. Emotional intelligence, which encompasses the ability to understand and manage one's own emotions and those of others, can impact decision-making by influencing how well individuals handle stress, conflict, and feedback. High emotional intelligence can lead to better interpersonal relationships and more effective team decisions.

Organizational Constraints and Decision Making

Organizational constraints are factors within the organization that can limit or influence decision-making processes. These constraints include organizational policies, resource limitations, time pressures, and hierarchical structures. For instance, strict organizational policies and procedures can limit the flexibility of decision-makers, forcing them to adhere to predefined guidelines even when a more adaptive approach might be beneficial. Resource limitations, such as budget constraints or lack of personnel, can restrict the range of options available and force managers to make trade-offs. Time pressures can lead to rushed decisions without thorough analysis, increasing the risk of errors. Additionally, hierarchical structures can affect decision-making by centralizing authority and limiting the input from lower-level employees, potentially stifacing creativity and innovation.

Integrating Individual Differences and Organizational Constraints in Decision Making

When individual differences and organizational constraints intersect, they create a complex environment for decision-making. A manager with high emotional intelligence and a preference for collaborative decision-making might struggle in a rigid hierarchical structure that values top-down directives. Conversely, an analytical thinker in a fast-paced environment with tight deadlines might find it challenging to gather and process all necessary data before making decisions. Recognizing these dynamics, effective leaders strive to balance individual and organizational factors by fostering a culture that values diverse perspectives and adaptive decision-making processes. This might involve creating cross-functional teams to leverage different cognitive styles and experiences or implementing flexible policies that allow for situational adjustments. By understanding and navigating the interplay between individual differences and organizational constraints, leaders can make more informed, balanced, and effective decisions that align with both personal strengths and organizational needs.

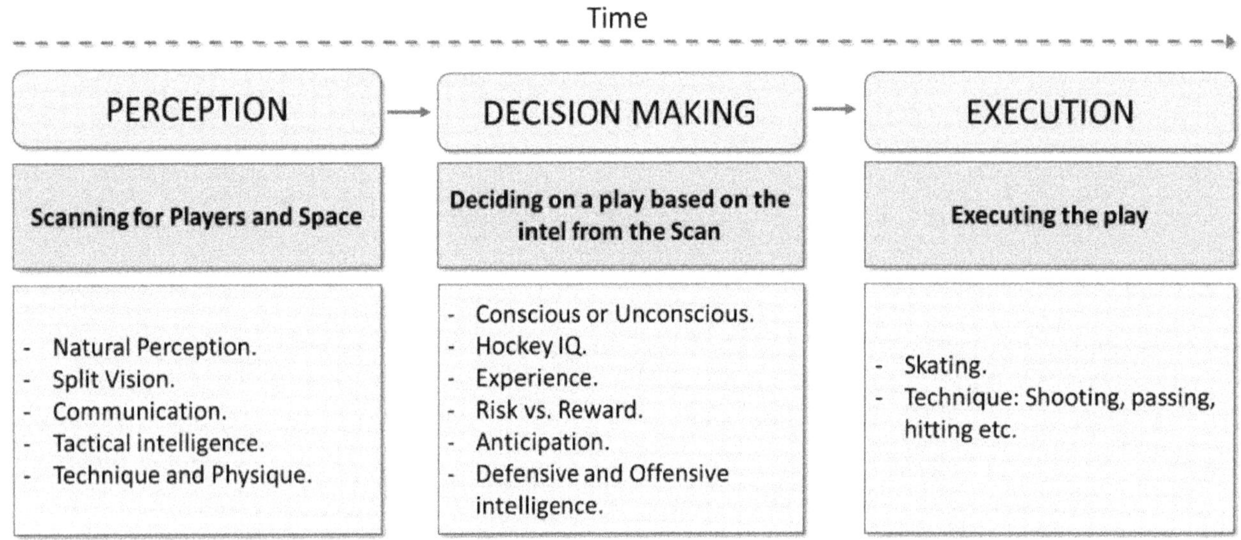

Integrating Perception, Decision Making, and Execution

Individual Differences and Execution

Execution, the process of carrying out plans and strategies, is greatly influenced by individual differences. Personality traits, work ethic, and personal skills all play critical roles in how effectively tasks are executed. For instance, individuals with high conscientiousness tend to be organized, dependable, and disciplined, which enhances their ability to follow through on tasks and meet deadlines. People with strong problem-solving skills can effectively navigate challenges and find solutions, ensuring smoother execution. Additionally, differences in motivation levels can impact execution; highly motivated individuals are likely to be more committed and put in extra effort to achieve their goals. Emotional intelligence also affects execution, as individuals who can manage their emotions and understand others' emotions can work better in teams, handle stress more effectively, and maintain a positive work environment.

Organizational Constraints and Execution

Organizational constraints significantly affect the execution of plans and strategies. These constraints can include structural factors, resource availability, organizational culture, and communication channels. Structural factors, such as bureaucratic processes and hierarchical layers, can slow down execution by requiring multiple approvals and creating bottlenecks.

Resource availability, including access to technology, financial resources, and skilled personnel, directly impacts the ability to execute tasks efficiently. Organizational culture plays a crucial role; a culture that fosters innovation, collaboration, and accountability can enhance execution, while a culture resistant to change or lacking clear communication can hinder it. Effective communication channels are essential for execution, as they ensure that all team members understand their roles, responsibilities, and deadlines, reducing the risk of misunderstandings and errors.

Integrating Individual Differences and Organizational Constraints in Execution

The interplay between individual differences and organizational constraints is crucial for effective execution. A highly motivated and skilled individual might still struggle to execute effectively if faced with significant organizational constraints, such as insufficient resources or a restrictive culture. Conversely, an organization with abundant resources and a supportive culture might not achieve optimal execution if the individuals involved lack the necessary skills or motivation. To navigate this interplay, leaders should focus on aligning individual capabilities with organizational support. This can involve providing training and development opportunities to enhance individual skills, creating a supportive culture that encourages initiative and accountability, and ensuring that resources are allocated efficiently. Additionally, fostering open communication and collaboration can help mitigate the impact of organizational constraints by leveraging the diverse strengths of team members. By addressing both individual and organizational factors, leaders can enhance execution, ensuring that plans and strategies are implemented effectively and goals are achieved.

Understanding Decision-Making Models in Organizations

- ***Role of Decision-Making Models***

Decision-making models provide structured frameworks for managers to analyze situations, evaluate alternatives, and make informed choices within organizations. These models guide managers through the complex process of decision-making, helping them consider relevant factors and weigh different options systematically. By understanding and applying decision-making models, managers can improve the quality of their decisions, enhance organizational outcomes, and mitigate risks.

- ***Types of Decision-Making Models***

Several decision-making models exist, each suited to different types of decisions and organizational contexts. One commonly used model is the rational decision-making model, which follows a logical sequence of steps: identifying the problem, gathering information, evaluating alternatives, making a choice, implementing the decision, and monitoring outcomes. This model assumes that decision-makers are rational and objective, aiming to maximize outcomes based on clear criteria.

Another model is the bounded rationality model, which acknowledges that decision-makers may have limited time, information, and cognitive resources. In this model, decision-makers satisfice rather than optimize, selecting the first satisfactory option that meets their needs rather than exhaustively evaluating all alternatives. This approach is more realistic in situations where time and resources are constrained, such as in fast-paced environments or when facing urgent decisions.

- ***Application of Decision-Making Models***

Managers apply decision-making models across various organizational functions, including strategic planning, resource allocation, risk management, and problem-solving. For example, when developing a new product strategy, managers might use the rational decision-making model to analyze market trends, evaluate competitors, and identify potential risks before making an informed choice. In contrast, when addressing an operational issue, such as equipment breakdowns on the production line, managers might employ the bounded rationality model to quickly assess available options and implement a solution to minimize downtime.

- ***Consideration of Individual and Organizational Factors***

Individual differences and organizational constraints also influence the application of decision-making models. Managers' cognitive styles, personality traits, and emotional intelligence affect how they interpret and implement decision-making models. For instance, a manager with a preference for analytical thinking might favor the rational decision-making model, while a manager with high emotional intelligence might prioritize consensus-building and stakeholder engagement.

Organizational factors such as culture, structure, and resource availability also shape decision-making processes. In a hierarchical organization with centralized decision-making authority, managers may adhere more closely to formal decision-making models, following prescribed procedures and seeking approval from higher levels. In contrast, in a decentralized organization with a culture of empowerment and innovation, managers may have more flexibility to adapt decision-making models to suit their unique needs and preferences.

- ***Integration of Decision-Making Models with Real-World Context***

In practice, effective managers integrate decision-making models with real-world context, combining theoretical frameworks with practical insights and experiential knowledge. This integration enables managers to adapt decision-making processes to dynamic and complex organizational environments, navigating uncertainty, ambiguity, and conflicting priorities effectively. By leveraging decision-making models alongside individual expertise and organizational dynamics, managers can make more informed, timely, and strategic decisions that drive organizational success.

Perceptions in the realam of Managerial Psychology

Perception is the process by which individuals organize and interpret their sensory impressions to give meaning to their environment. It plays a crucial role in the decision-making process, as it is through perception that we understand the information that influences our decisions. Understanding perception is vital for managers as it affects how problems are identified, alternatives are generated, and decisions are ultimately made within an organization.

Understanding Perception

Perception is a cognitive process that enables us to interpret and understand our surroundings. It involves the acquisition and processing of sensory information to see, hear, taste, or smell the world around us. The perception process consists of four stages: stimulus, sensation, attention, and interpretation. The process begins with the presence of stimuli in our environment that are available for our senses to detect. Our sensory organs then detect these stimuli and transmit the information to our brain. Our brain pays attention to certain stimuli while ignoring others based on factors such as intensity, contrast, and movement. Finally, our brain interprets these stimuli based on our past experiences, knowledge, and individual differences.

Perception in the Workplace

In the context of management, perception plays a vital role in various organizational processes such as decision making, leadership, communication, and motivation. Managers need to understand that employees may perceive the same situation differently, and these perceptions can significantly impact their attitudes and behaviors. For instance, a manager's feedback might be perceived as constructive criticism by one employee but as a personal attack by another. These differing perceptions can influence how employees react and perform in their roles. Therefore, effective communication and an awareness of perceptual differences are crucial for managers to foster a positive and productive work environment.

Decision Making Process

Decision making is a cognitive process that results in the selection of a course of action among several alternatives. It involves several steps: identifying the problem, generating alternatives, evaluating alternatives, choosing an alternative, implementing the decision, and evaluating the decision. The first step is to recognize that a problem exists. Once the problem is identified, possible solutions or alternatives are generated. Each alternative is then evaluated based on its potential to solve the problem. The best alternative is chosen based on this evaluation, and the chosen alternative is implemented to solve the problem. Finally, the effectiveness of the decision is evaluated to ensure that the desired outcome has been achieved.

Role of Perception in Decision Making

Perception influences decision making in several ways. It shapes our understanding of the problem, the generation and evaluation of alternatives, and our assessment of the decision's effectiveness. Perceptual biases can distort the decision-making process, leading to suboptimal outcomes. For instance, confirmation bias may lead managers to favor information that supports their existing beliefs while ignoring contradictory evidence. Anchoring bias might cause them to rely too heavily on the first piece of information encountered. Overconfidence bias can result in overestimating the accuracy of their decisions. Managers need to be aware of these biases and strive to mitigate their impact to make more objective and effective decisions.

Understanding the interplay between perception and decision making is crucial for effective management. By being aware of how perception influences decision making, managers can make better decisions and lead their organizations more effectively. Awareness of perceptual biases and fostering an environment where different perspectives are valued can help in making more informed and balanced decisions. This understanding can lead to better problem identification, more creative solutions, and a thorough evaluation of the decisions made, ultimately enhancing organizational performance.

Perception is the process by which individuals organize and interpret their sensory impressions to give meaning to their environment. It plays a crucial role in the decision-making process, as it is through perception that we understand the information that influences our decisions. Understanding perception is vital for managers as it affects how problems are identified, alternatives are generated, and decisions are ultimately made within an organization.

Understanding Perception

Perception is a cognitive process that enables us to interpret and understand our surroundings. It involves the acquisition and processing of sensory information to see, hear, taste, or smell the world around us. The perception process consists of four stages: stimulus, sensation, attention, and interpretation. The process begins with the presence of stimuli in our environment that are available for our senses to detect. Our sensory organs then detect these stimuli and transmit the information to our brain. Our brain pays attention to certain stimuli while ignoring others based on factors such as intensity, contrast, and movement. Finally, our brain interprets these stimuli based on our past experiences, knowledge, and individual differences.

Perception in the Workplace

In the context of management, perception plays a vital role in various organizational processes such as decision making, leadership, communication, and motivation. Managers need to understand that employees may perceive the same situation differently, and these perceptions can significantly impact their attitudes and behaviors. For instance, a manager's feedback might be perceived as constructive criticism by one employee but as a personal attack by another. These differing perceptions can influence how employees react and perform in their roles. Therefore, effective communication and an awareness of perceptual differences are crucial for managers to foster a positive and productive work environment.

Decision Making Process

Decision making is a cognitive process that results in the selection of a course of action among several alternatives. It involves several steps: identifying the problem, generating alternatives, evaluating alternatives, choosing an alternative, implementing the decision, and evaluating the decision. The first step is to recognize that a problem exists. Once the problem is identified, possible solutions or alternatives are generated. Each alternative is then evaluated based on its potential to solve the problem. The best alternative is chosen based on this evaluation, and the chosen alternative is implemented to solve the problem. Finally, the effectiveness of the decision is evaluated to ensure that the desired outcome has been achieved.

Role of Perception in Decision Making

Perception influences decision making in several ways. It shapes our understanding of the problem, the generation and evaluation of alternatives, and our assessment of the decision's effectiveness. Perceptual biases can distort the decision-making process, leading to suboptimal outcomes. For instance, confirmation bias may lead managers to favor information that supports their existing beliefs while ignoring contradictory evidence. Anchoring bias might cause them to rely too heavily on the first piece of information encountered. Overconfidence bias can result in overestimating the accuracy of their decisions. Managers need to be aware of these biases and strive to mitigate their impact to make more objective and effective decisions.

Understanding the interplay between perception and decision making is crucial for effective management. By being aware of how perception influences decision making, managers can make better decisions and lead their organizations more effectively. Awareness of perceptual biases and fostering an environment where different perspectives are valued can help in making more informed and balanced decisions. This understanding can lead to better problem identification, more creative solutions, and a thorough evaluation of the decisions made, ultimately enhancing organizational performance.

Questions:

1. *How does perception influence decision-making processes in the workplace? Provide examples of common perceptual biases that can affect managerial decisions.*

2. *Discuss the stages of the decision-making process. How can leaders ensure that they are making well-informed and objective decisions at each stage?*

3. *What is attribution theory, and how does it explain the way individuals interpret and assign causes to behaviors and events in the workplace? Give examples of how attributions*

can affect employee performance evaluations.

4. *How can the concept of execution be differentiated from decision-making? Discuss the importance of effective execution in achieving organizational goals and how leaders can bridge the gap between planning and implementation.*

5. *Explain the role of cognitive biases in the decision-making process. How can awareness of these biases improve the accuracy and fairness of managerial decisions? Provide examples of strategies to mitigate the impact of biases.*

CHAPTER SIX

Interpersonal Dynamics

"Teamwork begins by building trust. And the only way to do that is to overcome our need for invulnerability." — Patrick Lencioni

This quote by Patrick Lencioni highlights the importance of trust in interpersonal dynamics within teams. It emphasizes that genuine teamwork requires members to be open, honest, and vulnerable with each other, which fosters a strong foundation of trust. Interpersonal dynamics, the complex and nuanced interactions between individuals within various contexts, are at the heart of human relationships. These dynamics influence how we communicate, collaborate, and connect with others, impacting personal and professional environments alike. Understanding these interactions is crucial for anyone seeking to navigate social landscapes effectively, whether in personal relationships, workplace settings, or broader community interactions. This chapter delves into the fundamental aspects of interpersonal dynamics, exploring the psychological, social, and cultural factors that shape our interactions and relationships.

Interpersonal dynamics are a foundational element of human interaction, influencing every aspect of our lives. By understanding and improving these dynamics, we can build stronger, more meaningful relationships and create more harmonious and effective social and professional environments. This chapter aims to provide a comprehensive overview of the key concepts and practical strategies for enhancing interpersonal dynamics, equipping readers with the knowledge and skills needed to navigate the complexities of human relationships successfully. Through a deeper understanding of the psychological, social, and cultural factors that shape our interactions, we can foster better communication, collaboration, and connection in all areas of our lives.

The Importance of Interpersonal Dynamics

The study of interpersonal dynamics is essential because it helps us comprehend the underlying mechanisms that drive human behavior in social contexts. Effective interpersonal skills are critical for building and maintaining healthy relationships, resolving conflicts, and fostering cooperation. In the workplace, strong interpersonal dynamics contribute to team cohesion, employee satisfaction, and organizational success. By understanding the principles of interpersonal dynamics, individuals can enhance their communication skills, develop empathy, and improve their ability to influence and persuade others.

Psychological Foundations of Interpersonal Dynamics

At the core of interpersonal dynamics are psychological processes that govern how we perceive and respond to others. Factors such as personality traits, emotional intelligence, and cognitive biases play significant roles in shaping our interactions. For instance, individuals with high emotional intelligence are better equipped to recognize and manage their own emotions and those of others, leading to more effective and harmonious interactions. Additionally, understanding cognitive biases, such as confirmation bias or attribution error, can help individuals navigate misunderstandings and improve their decision-making processes in social contexts.

Social and Cultural Influences on Interpersonal Dynamics

Interpersonal dynamics are also profoundly influenced by social and cultural contexts. Social norms, cultural values, and societal expectations shape how we interact with others and interpret their behavior. For example, cultural differences in communication styles—such as the preference for direct versus indirect communication—can lead to misunderstandings in multicultural settings. By acknowledging and respecting these differences, individuals can foster more inclusive and respectful interactions. Moreover, societal structures and power dynamics, such as gender roles and hierarchical relationships, also impact interpersonal dynamics, influencing how authority, respect, and collaboration are negotiated in various contexts.

Enhancing Interpersonal Dynamics for Personal and Professional Growth

Developing strong interpersonal dynamics is a continuous process that requires self-awareness, practice, and a willingness to learn from experiences. Techniques such as active listening, effective feedback, and conflict resolution strategies are vital tools for improving interpersonal interactions. In professional settings, training programs focused on teamwork, leadership, and communication skills can significantly enhance interpersonal dynamics, leading to more productive and positive work environments. On a personal level, fostering authentic connections, practicing empathy, and being open to diverse perspectives can enrich our relationships and contribute to overall well-being.

Communication Skills for Managers

Effective communication skills are crucial for managers as they serve as the foundation for successful leadership and organizational effectiveness. Clear and concise communication enables managers to convey expectations, provide feedback, and align team efforts towards common goals. For instance, at Google, managers are trained to give clear and actionable feedback through regular one-on-one meetings. This practice not only enhances employee performance but also fosters a culture of transparency and trust within the team. Managers who communicate effectively can ensure that their teams understand their roles and responsibilities, leading to increased productivity and reduced misunderstandings.

Moreover, effective communication skills are essential for conflict resolution and maintaining a positive work environment. Managers often encounter conflicts arising from miscommunications or differing perspectives among team members. At Amazon, managers are encouraged to adopt a "disagree and commit" approach, where team members can voice their disagreements but are committed to the decision once it is made. This approach requires managers to facilitate open discussions and ensure that all voices are heard, thus preventing conflicts from escalating and maintaining team cohesion. By effectively managing conflicts through clear communication, managers can promote a collaborative atmosphere where issues are addressed constructively.

Effective communication is also vital for inspiring and motivating employees. Managers who can articulate a clear vision and provide regular updates on organizational goals can significantly boost team morale and engagement. For example, at Microsoft, CEO Satya Nadella's open communication style and emphasis on empathy have been credited with transforming the company's culture and driving innovation. Nadella's ability to communicate the company's mission and values has resonated with employees, leading to increased commitment and a stronger sense of purpose. Managers who communicate effectively can inspire their teams to achieve higher performance levels and contribute to the organization's overall success.

Verbal and Non-verbal Communication

Effective communication encompasses both verbal and nonverbal elements, each playing a crucial role in conveying messages accurately and fostering understanding between individuals. Verbal communication involves the use of spoken or written words to convey information, while nonverbal communication includes body language, facial expressions, gestures, tone of voice, and other subtle cues.

Verbal communication allows individuals to articulate thoughts, ideas, and information clearly and directly. It involves choosing the right words, using appropriate language, and structuring sentences effectively to ensure that messages are conveyed accurately. For example, in a business meeting, a manager may use verbal communication to provide instructions to team members, deliver presentations, or facilitate discussions on project objectives. Clear and concise verbal communication helps to avoid misunderstandings, promotes transparency, and ensures that everyone is on the same page.

Nonverbal communication, on the other hand, complements verbal messages and provides additional context and meaning to the conversation. Body language, such as posture, facial expressions, eye contact, and hand gestures, can convey emotions, attitudes, and intentions more vividly than words alone. For instance, during a job interview, a candidate's nonverbal cues, such as maintaining eye contact, smiling, and sitting upright, can communicate confidence, professionalism, and interest in the position. Managers must pay attention to nonverbal signals both in themselves and others to better understand underlying emotions and attitudes and respond appropriately.

Effective communication occurs when verbal and nonverbal elements align to create a cohesive message. In interpersonal interactions, inconsistencies between verbal and nonverbal cues can lead to confusion or mistrust. For example, if a manager praises an employee's performance verbally but displays negative body language, such as crossed arms or a frown, the employee may perceive mixed messages and feel uncertain about their performance. Therefore, mastering both verbal and nonverbal communication skills is essential for building rapport, fostering trust, and establishing effective relationships in both personal and professional settings.

Active Listening Techniques

Active listening is a fundamental skill that enhances communication and strengthens relationships by demonstrating genuine interest and empathy towards the speaker. Here are some key techniques for practicing active listening:

Pay Attention: *Give the speaker your full attention by maintaining eye contact, facing them directly, and minimizing distractions. Show interest through nonverbal cues such as nodding and leaning forward.*

Paraphrase and Summarize: *Reflect back on what the speaker has said by paraphrasing their message in your own words. Summarize key points to demonstrate understanding and ensure clarity.*

Ask Open-Ended Questions: *Encourage the speaker to elaborate on their thoughts and feelings by asking open-ended questions that invite detailed responses. Avoid interrupting or jumping to conclusions.*

Provide Feedback: *Offer feedback to the speaker to validate their feelings and experiences. Use affirming statements such as "I understand," "That must have been difficult," or "Thank you for sharing."*

Empathize: *Put yourself in the speaker's shoes and try to understand their perspective and emotions. Show empathy by acknowledging their feelings and expressing understanding without judgment.*

Avoid Judgment and Assumptions: *Suspend judgment and refrain from making assumptions or jumping to conclusions about the speaker's motives or intentions. Stay neutral and noncritical.*

Maintain Silence: Allow moments of silence to give the speaker time to collect their thoughts and express themselves fully. Avoid filling the silence with your own thoughts or responses.

Reflect Feelings: *Acknowledge the speaker's emotions and validate their experiences by reflecting their feelings back to them. Use phrases like "It sounds like you're feeling..." or "I sense that you're..."*

Focus on the Speaker: *Resist the urge to redirect the conversation back to yourself or offer unsolicited advice. Keep the focus on the speaker's needs and concerns.*

Show Respect: *Demonstrate respect for the speaker's opinions, even if you disagree. Avoid interrupting or dominating the conversation and allow them to speak without feeling rushed.*

By practicing active listening techniques, you can foster stronger connections, improve understanding, and build trust in your interpersonal relationships.

Receiving and Giving Feedback

In corporate settings, effective feedback is instrumental in driving performance, enhancing teamwork, and achieving organizational goals. For example, consider a scenario where a manager provides feedback to a sales representative on their client presentation skills. Instead of simply stating, "Your presentation was weak," the manager could use the SBI model to offer more constructive feedback. They might say, "During yesterday's client meeting (Situation), I noticed that you struggled to maintain eye contact and spoke too quickly (Behavior). This may have led to some confusion among the clients and impacted their perception of our proposal (Impact). To improve, I suggest practicing your delivery pace and incorporating more visual aids to engage the audience effectively."

Moreover, regular and timely feedback can significantly impact employee engagement and motivation. For instance, imagine a team leader who conducts weekly feedback sessions with their direct reports to discuss project progress and address any challenges or concerns. By providing ongoing feedback and support, the leader enables team members to identify areas for improvement, celebrate successes, and collaborate more effectively. This proactive approach to feedback fosters a culture of transparency, accountability, and continuous learning within the team, ultimately driving performance and achieving organizational objectives.

Furthermore, effective feedback mechanisms are essential for fostering innovation and driving organizational change. For instance, consider a company that solicits feedback from employees through regular surveys, focus groups, and suggestion boxes. By actively seeking input from employees at all levels of the organization, the company can identify areas for improvement, uncover innovative ideas, and address potential issues before they escalate. This inclusive approach to feedback not only empowers employees to contribute to the company's success but also promotes a sense of ownership and belonging, driving overall organizational performance and competitiveness in the marketplace.

Improving interpersonal dynamics is essential for managers and leaders to effectively lead and collaborate with their teams. Here are five important suggestions focusing on communication skills:

Develop Verbal and Non-Verbal Communication Skills: Managers should hone their ability to articulate ideas clearly and concisely, both verbally and non-verbally. This includes maintaining eye contact, using appropriate body language, and speaking with confidence and authority. By mastering these skills, managers can convey their messages more effectively and build rapport with their team members.

Practice Active Listening Techniques: Active listening is a crucial skill for managers to understand their team members' perspectives, concerns, and ideas. This involves giving full attention to the speaker, paraphrasing and summarizing their points, and asking clarifying questions. By actively listening, managers demonstrate empathy, foster trust, and create an open communication environment where everyone feels valued and heard.

Master Giving and Receiving Feedback: Effective feedback is essential for continuous improvement and performance management. Managers should provide timely, specific, and constructive feedback to their team members, focusing on behaviors rather than personalities. Similarly, managers should be open to receiving feedback from their team members, demonstrating humility and a willingness to learn and grow. By fostering a culture of feedback, managers can encourage self-reflection, skill development, and accountability within their teams.

Lead by Example: Managers should lead by example when it comes to interpersonal dynamics and communication skills. They should model the behaviors they expect from their team members, such as active listening, respectful communication, and openness to feedback. By demonstrating these behaviors consistently, managers set a positive tone for their teams and inspire trust and collaboration.

Invest in Training and Development: Finally, managers should invest in their own training and development to continuously enhance their interpersonal skills. This may involve attending workshops or seminars on communication, conflict resolution, emotional intelligence, or leadership development. By investing in their own growth, managers can become more effective communicators and leaders, ultimately driving team performance and success.

Questions:

1. *How do effective interpersonal behaviors contribute to a positive workplace culture? Discuss specific behaviors that enhance teamwork and collaboration.*

2. *What are the key components of active listening, and how can improving this skill enhance communication between team members and leaders in the workplace?*

3. *Discuss the role of clear and effective communication in preventing misunderstandings and conflicts at work. Provide examples of strategies that can be employed to improve communication in diverse teams.*

4. *How can constructive feedback be delivered in a way that motivates and engages employees rather than discourages them? Outline best practices for giving and receiving feedback.*

5. *Explain the impact of non-verbal communication on workplace interactions. How can an awareness of body language and facial expressions improve the effectiveness of workplace communication?*

40

CHAPTER SEVEN

Conflict Resolution and Negotiation

"Conflict is inevitable, but combat is optional." — Max Lucado

This quote by Max Lucado highlights the idea that while disagreements and conflicts are a natural part of human interaction, how we respond to them is a choice. Effective conflict management involves addressing issues constructively rather than allowing them to escalate into unproductive or harmful confrontations. Conflict resolution and negotiation are integral aspects of managerial psychology, playing pivotal roles in organizational dynamics and decision-making processes. In this chapter, we delve into the intricate interplay between individuals and groups, exploring the psychology behind conflicts and negotiations in professional settings. From understanding the root causes of conflicts to mastering negotiation strategies, managers need to navigate complex interpersonal dynamics to foster collaboration, mitigate disputes, and achieve organizational goals.

Conflict is inevitable in any workplace, stemming from differences in personalities, priorities, goals, and values among team members. By examining the psychological factors underlying conflicts, managers can gain insights into how to address and manage them effectively. Additionally, negotiation skills are indispensable for resolving conflicts and reaching mutually beneficial agreements. Whether it's bargaining with stakeholders, mediating disputes between colleagues, or brokering deals with clients, managers must leverage negotiation techniques to navigate diverse interests and achieve win-win outcomes.

Drawing on principles from psychology, sociology, and organizational behavior, this chapter provides a comprehensive framework for understanding conflict resolution and negotiation in managerial contexts. We explore various conflict resolution models, such as the Thomas-Kilmann Conflict Mode Instrument (TKI), which categorizes conflict-handling styles based on assertiveness and cooperativeness. Moreover, we delve into the psychology of negotiation, examining concepts like BATNA (Best Alternative to a Negotiated Agreement), anchoring effects, and integrative bargaining strategies.

Through real-world case studies and practical examples, we illustrate how effective conflict resolution and negotiation skills can enhance organizational performance and foster positive workplace relationships. From resolving interpersonal conflicts to negotiating strategic alliances, managers must navigate a myriad of challenges with finesse and diplomacy. By mastering the principles outlined in this chapter, managers can cultivate a culture of collaboration, creativity, and constructive problem-solving, ultimately driving success in today's dynamic business environment.

Conflict Resolution Models

Thomas-Kilmann Conflict Mode Instrument (TKI) *is a widely used tool for assessing individuals' preferred approaches to handling conflicts. Developed by psychologists Kenneth W. Thomas and Ralph H. Kilmann, the TKI measures five distinct conflict-handling styles based on varying degrees of assertiveness and cooperativeness. These styles include competing, collaborating, compromising, avoiding, and accommodating.*

Competing *is characterized by high assertiveness and low cooperativeness, where individuals prioritize their own needs and objectives over others'. This approach may be appropriate in situations requiring quick decisions or when standing up for important principles. Individuals who compete can be assertive and uncooperative. They value their own goals over the goals of others. They may view being right as more important than preserving the relationship with the other party.*

When to use:

- *A quick, decisive action is required, such as in an emergency situation.*
- *You are certain that you are correct /or that it's in the best interest of all parties involved.*

Collaborating *involves high assertiveness and high cooperativeness, emphasizing open communication and problem-solving to reach mutually beneficial solutions. This style is ideal for resolving complex issues and building strong relationships among team members. Individuals who collaborate use a combination of being assertive and cooperative to work with others to find solutions that are beneficial to everyone. These individuals see conflict as an opportunity to improve relationships and reduce tensions.*

When to use:

- *The concerns of everyone involved are of utmost importance.*
- *There is a high degree of trust among everyone involved in the conflict.*

Compromising *strikes a balance between assertiveness and cooperativeness, with individuals seeking moderate gains for both parties through concessions and trade-offs. Compromising is useful when time constraints or limited resources necessitate swift resolution. Compromise is both sides willing to give up something to gain something in return: a middle ground between two positions. Individuals with this style are willing to sacrifice some in order to find an agreement.*

When to use:

- *The people who are in conflict are willing to be flexible.*
- *The affected individuals will be satisfied with getting part of what they want.*
- *As a back-up plan for collaboration, in situations where a win-win outcome isn't possible.*

Avoiding *reflects low assertiveness and low cooperativeness, as individuals sidestep conflicts or postpone resolution in favor of maintaining harmony or avoiding confrontation. While avoiding can provide temporary relief, it may not address underlying issues and can lead to unresolved tensions. These individuals may step away from a situation to gain clarity. This may even include giving up their goals or relationships to avoid conflict. "Perhaps if we don't bring it up, it will blow over"*

When to use:

- *You need time to think through the situation before moving forward with a resolution.*
- *The issue is one that is so trivial there is no point in putting time and energy into dealing with it.*

***Accommodating** entails low assertiveness and high cooperativeness, where individuals prioritize the needs and interests of others over their own. This approach fosters goodwill and can be beneficial in preserving relationships or de-escalating conflicts. Individuals who accommodate may put the needs of others before their own. These individuals generally value their relationships over their own goals, but almost never leave a conflict satisfied.*

When to use:

- *The issue is trivial, and the outcome really doesn't matter.*
- *Harmony is actually more important than resolving the situation that is in conflict.*
- *It's important to let the other person learn from their own mistakes.*

The TKI assessment provides individuals and teams with valuable insights into their preferred conflict-handling styles and how they can adapt their approaches to different situations. By understanding the strengths and limitations of each style, individuals can make informed choices to effectively manage conflicts and achieve positive outcomes in diverse organizational contexts.

Three categories of conflict resolution

Conflict resolution can also be categorized into three types that can be used independently or together:

1. *Third-party intervention*
2. *Unilateral decision-making*
3. *Joint decision-making*

Third-party intervention *in conflict resolution involves the involvement of a neutral party to facilitate communication, negotiation, and resolution between conflicting parties. This intervention can take various forms, such as mediation, arbitration, or facilitation, depending on the nature and complexity of the conflict. The third party acts as a neutral mediator or facilitator, guiding the parties through the conflict resolution process while ensuring fairness, impartiality, and confidentiality. By providing an external perspective and helping parties explore their interests, concerns, and underlying needs, third-party intervention can help bridge communication gaps, reduce hostility, and foster collaborative problem-solving.*

Unilateral decision-making *occurs when one party in a conflict unilaterally imposes a decision or solution without the input or agreement of the other party. While this approach may lead to expedited decision-making and resolution in certain situations, it can also exacerbate tensions, breed resentment, and undermine trust and cooperation between parties. Unilateral decision-making may be necessary in emergencies or when immediate action is required, but it is generally less effective in fostering long-term relationships and sustainable solutions. Moreover, it often neglects the interests and perspectives of the other party, potentially perpetuating or escalating the conflict.*

Joint decision-making*, on the other hand, involves collaborative efforts between conflicting parties to jointly identify, evaluate, and agree upon solutions that meet the needs and interests of all stakeholders. This approach prioritizes open communication, active listening, and mutual respect, allowing parties to explore creative options, build consensus, and share ownership of the decision-making process and outcomes. Joint decision-making fosters trust, cooperation, and commitment among parties, leading to more durable agreements and sustainable resolutions. While it may require more time, effort, and compromise, joint decision-making promotes mutual understanding and lays the foundation for constructive relationships and future collaboration.*

Many common mental and emotional patterns, often unconscious, can make conflicts worse, requiring conflict resolution methods to reach an agreement. People in a conflict usually believe they are right and the other side is wrong because they struggle to see things from the other's perspective. This bias is known as egocentrism.

One way to resolve such a deadlock, suggested by conflict resolution theory, is to create a positive atmosphere by allowing the other person to speak first. When it's your turn, insist on sharing your view without interruptions. Focus on explaining your perspective clearly, using evidence if needed.

Another strategy from conflict resolution theory is to involve a mediator. A mediator is a neutral third party who helps both sides reach a consensus. Instead of deciding the outcome, a mediator encourages both parties to explore their underlying interests. They work with the parties together and separately to help them find a resolution that is fair, voluntary, and nonbinding.

Conflict Management Styles Assessment

There are five core conflict management styles: Competing, Collaborating, Avoiding, Accommodating, and Compromising. Do you know which one you utilize most often when approached with a conflict? Take this 15-question assessment to figure it out.

Keep in mind that one style of conflict management is not necessarily better than another; each style has pros and cons, and each can be useful depending on the situation. This assessment is intended to help you identify your typical response to conflict, with the goal that when you encounter future conflicts, you will be aware of not only your instinctive reaction, but also the pros and cons of that reaction for the specific situation. Furthermore, you will also be aware of the other styles of conflict management that you could draw on to resolve the situation, if one of the other styles is more appropriate for the current situation.

To what extent does each statement describe you? Please read each statement and write down a response from 1 (rarely) to 5 (always) that best describes you. Make sure to keep track of your answers as you will need the numbers to find out your style! Be honest - this survey is designed to help you learn about your conflict management style. There are no right or wrong answers!

In the past 6 months, how often did you do the following to handle conflicts?

1. *If someone disagrees with me, I vigorously defend my side of the issue.*

2. *I go along with suggestions from peers, even if I don't agree with them.*

3. *I give-and-take so that an agreement can be reached.*

4. *I keep my opinions to myself rather than openly disagree with people.*

5.
In disagreements or negotiations, I try to find the best possible solutions for both sides by sharing information.

6.
I try to reach a middle ground in disputes with other people.

7.
I go along with the wishes of people who have different points of view than my own.

8.
I refrain from openly debating issues where there is disagreement.

9.
In negotiations, I hold on to my position rather than give in.

10.
I try to solve conflicts by finding solutions that benefit both me and the other person.

11.
I let peers have their way rather than jeopardize our relationship.

12.
I try to win my position in a discussion.

13.
I investigate conflicts with peers so that we can discover solutions that benefit both of us.

14.
It is not worth the time and trouble discussing my differences of opinion with other people.

15.
To reach an agreement, I give up some things in exchange for others.

As stated, the 15 statements correspond to the five approaches to conflict management. To find your most preferred style, total the points for each. The one with the highest score indicates your most commonly used strategy. The one with the lowest score indicates your least preferred strategy. However, all styles have pros and cons, so it's important that you can use the most appropriate style for each conflict situation.

Competing (1)________ + (9)_________ + (12)________ = ____________

Accommodating (2)_________ + (7)________ + (11)_________ = ____________

Compromising (3)_________ + (6)________ + (15)_________ = ____________

Avoiding (4)________ + (8)_______ + (14)________ = ___________

Collaborating (5)________ + (10)_______ + (13)________ = ___________

Remember the style with the highest score is the way in which you approach conflict most often. The styles listed below range on a scale from most assertive to most cooperative.

Conflict Management Styles

Psychology of Negotiation

Negotiation is a fundamental aspect of human interaction, influencing relationships in various contexts, including business, politics, and personal life. In the corporate world, negotiation skills are paramount for successful outcomes in dealing with clients, customers, and employees. For instance, when negotiating with clients, companies must strike a balance between meeting client demands and protecting their own interests. This requires understanding the client's needs, preferences, and constraints while also advocating for favorable terms for the company.

In customer negotiations, businesses often encounter diverse preferences and expectations, requiring adaptive negotiation strategies. For example, in retail settings, sales professionals negotiate with customers on pricing, product features, and service offerings to ensure customer satisfaction while maximizing profitability. Effective negotiation skills enable sales teams to build rapport, address customer concerns, and close deals that benefit both parties.

Negotiating with employees is equally critical for organizational success, particularly in matters such as compensation, performance evaluations, and conflict resolution. For instance, during salary negotiations, managers must balance budgetary constraints with fair compensation practices to retain top talent and maintain employee morale. Likewise, negotiation skills are essential for resolving interpersonal conflicts and promoting a positive work environment conducive to productivity and collaboration.

Moreover, the psychology of negotiation underscores the importance of factors such as communication, trust, and power dynamics in shaping negotiation outcomes. Research in this field highlights the role of emotions, cognitive biases, and cultural differences in influencing negotiation strategies and decision-making processes. By understanding these psychological principles, negotiators can adapt their approaches, build rapport, and leverage opportunities for mutually beneficial agreements in diverse negotiation contexts.

The Art and Science of Negotiation

The art and science of negotiation encapsulates both the strategic application of techniques and the nuanced interpersonal skills required to navigate complex bargaining situations effectively. While negotiation involves structured processes and analytical decision-making, it also relies on creativity, empathy, and intuition to achieve optimal outcomes for all parties involved.

At its core, negotiation is about reaching agreements that satisfy the interests of both sides while addressing conflicting needs and priorities. This delicate balance requires negotiators to deploy a blend of analytical thinking and emotional intelligence to understand the underlying motivations, concerns, and constraints of the parties at the table.

Negotiation encompasses a wide range of scenarios, from high-stakes business deals to everyday interactions where individuals seek to find common ground and resolve differences. Whether negotiating a multimillion-dollar contract or mediating a dispute between colleagues, mastering the art and science of negotiation empowers individuals to navigate conflicts, build relationships, and create value in diverse contexts.

Moreover, negotiation is a dynamic process shaped by cultural norms, power dynamics, and situational factors that influence the bargaining environment. Successful negotiators possess the flexibility to adapt their strategies and tactics to different situations, leveraging their knowledge of human behavior and communication techniques to foster collaboration and achieve win-win outcomes.

Ultimately, the art and science of negotiation represent a multifaceted skill set that combines analytical rigor, interpersonal finesse, and strategic thinking. By honing these capabilities, individuals can enhance their effectiveness as negotiators, unlocking opportunities for mutual gain and fostering positive outcomes in both professional and personal spheres.

***BATNA** (Best Alternative to a Negotiated Agreement)*

BATNA, or Best Alternative to a Negotiated Agreement, is a concept in negotiation theory that represents the course of action a party can take if the current negotiation fails to reach a satisfactory agreement. Developed by Roger Fisher and William Ury in their seminal book "Getting to Yes: Negotiating Agreement Without Giving In," BATNA serves as a critical benchmark for assessing the value of potential agreements and making informed decisions during negotiations.

A party's BATNA is essentially its fallback position—the alternative option or course of action that it can pursue if no agreement is reached. Understanding and evaluating BATNA is essential because it provides negotiators with leverage, empowering them to negotiate from a position of strength and make strategic decisions based on their alternatives.

For example, if a company is negotiating a contract with a supplier and has a strong BATNA of sourcing the same materials from another supplier at a lower cost, it can negotiate more aggressively with its current supplier, knowing that it has a viable alternative if the negotiations fail to produce favorable terms.

Assessing BATNA involves identifying and evaluating all available alternatives, considering factors such as cost, time, feasibility, and potential risks associated with each option. A strong BATNA enhances a negotiator's bargaining power by providing leverage and reducing dependence on reaching an agreement at any cost.

In practice, negotiators aim to improve their BATNA by exploring and developing alternative options before entering into negotiations. By investing time and effort in researching and cultivating backup plans, negotiators can strengthen their positions, increase their negotiating power, and improve their ability to achieve favorable outcomes in negotiations.

BATNA, or Best Alternative to a Negotiated Agreement, is a fundamental concept in negotiation theory introduced by Roger Fisher and William Ury in their book "Getting to Yes." It represents the most advantageous course of action a party can take if negotiations fail and an agreement cannot be reached. Understanding and developing your BATNA is crucial as it provides leverage in negotiations and helps you make informed decisions.

Step-by-Step Process:

Identify Your Alternatives:

Begin by brainstorming all possible alternatives to the current negotiation. These alternatives can include different suppliers, contracts, partners, or even walking away from the negotiation entirely.

List out these alternatives without evaluating them initially to ensure a comprehensive understanding of your options.

Evaluate Each Alternative:

Assess each alternative's feasibility, costs, benefits, and risks. This evaluation should be as objective as possible and may involve gathering additional data or consulting with experts.

Consider factors such as financial implications, timeframes, resources required, and potential outcomes for each alternative.

Determine the Best Alternative:

Compare the alternatives based on your evaluation. The best alternative is the one that provides the most benefits and the least costs and risks.

This best alternative becomes your BATNA. It's essential to be realistic and honest in this assessment to ensure your BATNA is robust and achievable.

Calculate Your Reservation Value:

Your reservation value is the least favorable point at which you are willing to accept a deal. It is directly linked to your BATNA.

If a proposed agreement is better than your BATNA, you should consider accepting it. If not, you should reject it and pursue your BATNA.

Prepare to Communicate Your BATNA:

While it's not always necessary to reveal your BATNA to the other party, being aware of it helps you negotiate from a position of strength.

In some cases, strategically disclosing your BATNA can pressure the other party to make a better offer. However, this should be done carefully to avoid undermining your position.

Update and Reassess:

Your BATNA can change as new information becomes available or circumstances evolve. Regularly update your BATNA to ensure it remains relevant.

Reassessing your BATNA during the negotiation process allows you to adapt your strategy and make more informed decisions.

Importance in Negotiation:

Leverage and Power:

Knowing your BATNA gives you leverage in negotiations. It ensures that you don't agree to unfavorable terms out of desperation or lack of options.

It empowers you to negotiate confidently, knowing that you have a solid fallback plan.

Decision-Making:

A clear BATNA helps in making rational decisions. It provides a benchmark against which you can evaluate offers and proposals from the other party.

This clarity prevents you from accepting a deal that is worse than your best alternative.

Risk Management:

Understanding your BATNA helps manage risks. It allows you to identify when it's better to walk away rather than agreeing to a suboptimal deal.

This approach reduces the likelihood of regrettable decisions and helps in achieving long-term negotiation goals.

Developing and understanding your BATNA is a critical scientific process in negotiation. It involves identifying, evaluating, and selecting the best alternatives to your current negotiation position. By knowing your BATNA, you gain leverage, make informed decisions, and manage risks effectively. Regularly reassessing your BATNA ensures that you remain adaptable and resilient in negotiations, ultimately leading to better outcomes and stronger agreements.

Effective Negotiation Techniques for Employees and Managers

Preparation and Research: *Before entering any negotiation, thorough preparation is crucial. This includes researching the other party's needs, goals, and constraints, as well as understanding your own objectives and limitations. For employees and managers, this means knowing the market standards for salaries, benefits, or other negotiation topics, and having a clear idea of what you are willing to accept and where you can be flexible. Detailed preparation can reveal common ground and potential trade-offs, making the negotiation smoother and more productive.*

Clear Objectives: *Both employees and managers should enter negotiations with clear, specific objectives. This involves setting realistic and achievable goals, such as a desired salary increase or project deadline extension. Clarity in your objectives helps in maintaining focus during the negotiation and prevents you from getting sidetracked by less important issues. Clearly defined goals also make it easier to measure the success of the negotiation.*

Active Listening: *Active listening is a vital technique in negotiation, as it helps build rapport and trust. By genuinely listening to the other party's concerns and needs, you can better understand their position and find mutually beneficial solutions. For managers, this means paying close attention to employees' career aspirations and personal circumstances. For employees, it means understanding the broader organizational goals and constraints.*

Effective Communication: *Articulate your points clearly and concisely. Effective communication involves not only speaking clearly but also using non-verbal cues such as body language and eye contact. Both employees and managers should practice articulating their positions in a way that is assertive yet respectful, ensuring that their message is understood without coming across as aggressive or confrontational.*

Building Relationships: *Building and maintaining good relationships can significantly impact the outcome of a negotiation. Trust and respect between parties can lead to more open and honest communication, making it easier to reach an agreement. For managers, fostering a positive relationship with employees can lead to more cooperative and productive negotiations. For employees, showing respect and professionalism can enhance their credibility and bargaining power.*

Flexibility and Creativity: *Flexibility in negotiations allows for creative problem-solving. Being open to alternative solutions that you may not have initially considered can lead to a win-win outcome. Employees and managers should be willing to explore different options and make concessions where appropriate, as long as the core objectives are met. This flexibility often results in innovative agreements that satisfy both parties.*

Understanding BATNA: *Knowing your Best Alternative to a Negotiated Agreement (BATNA) is crucial. This concept helps you determine the lowest acceptable value you are willing to accept. For employees, a strong BATNA might be another job offer, while for managers, it could be the availability of other qualified candidates. Understanding your BATNA provides leverage and ensures that you do not settle for a suboptimal agreement.*

Emotional Intelligence: *High emotional intelligence enables you to manage your emotions and understand the emotions of others. This is essential in maintaining a calm and composed demeanor during negotiations, even when discussions become intense. Managers should be empathetic to employees' concerns, while employees should remain professional and composed, avoiding emotional reactions that could undermine their position.*

Patience and Timing: *Patience is a key virtue in negotiations. Rushing the process can lead to mistakes and missed opportunities. Understanding the right timing to make proposals and concessions can also be strategic. Both employees and managers should be prepared to take breaks if negotiations become heated, allowing time for reflection and preventing impulsive* *decisions.*

Documentation and Follow-Up: *Once an agreement is reached, it is important to document the terms clearly. This prevents misunderstandings and ensures that both parties are held accountable. Following up on the implementation of the agreed terms is equally important to maintain trust and ensure that the negotiation leads to long-term satisfaction. For managers, this might mean regularly checking in on project progress, while for employees, it could involve confirming the details of new roles or responsibilities in writing.*

By incorporating these techniques, both employees and managers can navigate negotiations more effectively, fostering a collaborative environment that leads to mutually beneficial outcomes.

Questions:

1. *What are the most common sources of conflict in the workplace, and what strategies can managers use to effectively resolve these conflicts while maintaining a positive work environment?*

2. *Describe the key stages of the negotiation process. How can understanding these stages help negotiators achieve more favorable outcomes in organizational settings?*

3. *What is BATNA, and why is it a critical concept in negotiation? Provide examples of how identifying and leveraging one's BATNA can influence the negotiation process and outcomes.*

4. *How can organizations foster a culture of constructive conflict resolution? Discuss the role of training and policies in equipping employees with the skills needed to manage and resolve conflicts effectively.*

5. *In what ways can integrative negotiation techniques benefit both parties in a negotiation? Provide examples of how these techniques can lead to win-win solutions in organizational contexts.*

CHAPTER EIGHT

Building and Leading Effective Teams

"Great teams are not born, they're built. And they're built on a foundation of trust, shared vision, and a commitment to each other's success."

This quote emphasizes the active process of building effective teams. It highlights the key elements necessary for success, including trust, a common vision, and mutual support among team members. Effective leaders understand the importance of nurturing these qualities to cultivate high-performing teams. In today's dynamic and interconnected work environment, the ability to build and lead effective teams is paramount for organizational success. Teams have become the cornerstone of modern businesses, as they harness diverse skills, perspectives, and talents to tackle complex challenges and drive innovation. However, creating and managing a high-performing team is no small feat. It requires astute leadership, clear communication, and a deep understanding of group dynamics.

This chapter delves into the fundamental principles of building and leading effective teams. We explore strategies for assembling diverse teams, fostering collaboration, and cultivating a culture of trust and accountability. Additionally, we examine the role of leadership in guiding teams towards shared goals, navigating conflicts, and leveraging individual strengths. By mastering the art of team building and leadership, organizations can unlock the full potential of their workforce and achieve remarkable results in today's competitive landscape.

Understanding the Team: Exploring Psychological Aspects

Understanding the dynamics of a team involves delving into the intricate web of human psychology that shapes group behavior and performance. At the core of any team are individuals with unique personalities, motivations, and communication styles. Recognizing and appreciating these differences is essential for fostering cohesion and maximizing collective potential.

1.

Individual Differences and Team Composition: Teams are comprised of individuals with diverse backgrounds, experiences, and skills. These differences bring richness to the team but can also lead to friction if not managed effectively. Personality traits, such as extroversion, conscientiousness, and openness to experience, play a significant role in how individuals interact within a team. Understanding these traits can help team leaders leverage complementary strengths and mitigate potential conflicts. Moreover, factors such as gender, cultural background, and generational differences influence communication styles and decision-making processes within the team. By embracing diversity and promoting inclusivity, teams can harness the full spectrum of talents and perspectives to achieve collective goals.

2.

Group Dynamics and Social Identity: Group dynamics shape the way individuals perceive themselves and others within the team. Social identity theory posits that individuals derive part of their self-concept from their membership in social groups, including teams and organizations. This sense of identity influences how team members interact, collaborate, and align themselves with the team's objectives. Group cohesion, a sense of belonging, and shared norms and values are essential elements that bind team members together and foster a supportive environment. However, groupthink, conformity pressures, and ingroup biases can also hinder creativity and independent thinking within the team. Effective team leaders are mindful of these dynamics and strive to create an inclusive culture that encourages diverse perspectives and constructive dissent.

3.

Communication and Collaboration: Effective communication lies at the heart of successful teamwork. Clear, open, and honest communication channels facilitate the exchange of ideas, feedback, and information among team members. However, communication breakdowns, misunderstandings, and conflicts are common challenges that teams encounter. Psychological factors such as communication apprehension, attribution biases, and perceptual filters can impede effective communication within the team. Active listening, empathy, and assertive communication techniques are essential skills that team members can cultivate to overcome these barriers. Moreover, fostering a culture of psychological safety, where team members feel comfortable expressing their thoughts and opinions without fear of reprisal, is crucial for promoting open communication and collaboration.

4.

Leadership and Team Dynamics: Leadership plays a pivotal role in shaping team dynamics and performance. Effective leaders understand the psychological needs and motivations of team members and adapt their leadership style accordingly. Transformational leaders inspire and empower their teams by articulating a compelling vision, providing support and encouragement, and fostering a sense of collective purpose. Additionally, situational leadership theories emphasize the importance of flexibility and adaptability in leadership approaches, as different situations and team compositions may require varying degrees of directive or participative leadership. Moreover, leaders must navigate team conflicts, manage power dynamics, and promote accountability while fostering a culture of trust and respect. By cultivating strong interpersonal relationships and leading by example, leaders can create a positive team climate that fosters collaboration, innovation, and high performance.

In essence, understanding the psychological aspects of team dynamics is essential for building cohesive, high-performing teams. By recognizing individual differences, fostering a sense of belonging, promoting effective communication, and providing effective leadership, teams can harness the collective talents and energies of their members to achieve shared objectives and drive organizational success.

Understanding Team Formation: Unraveling the Psychological Dynamics

Team formation marks the inception of a group's journey toward shared goals and collective achievements. This process is not merely about assembling individuals but involves complex psychological dynamics that shape group identity, cohesion, and productivity.

1. *Forming: Establishing the Foundation: The forming stage marks the initial gathering of individuals into a team. At this stage, team members are often polite and cautious as they get acquainted with one another and clarify the team's purpose and objectives. Individuals may feel a sense of uncertainty and ambiguity about their roles and responsibilities within the team. Psychological factors such as social identity and self-disclosure play a crucial role in establishing rapport and trust among team members. Team leaders can facilitate this process by providing clarity on goals, setting expectations, and creating opportunities for team members to bond and build relationships.*

2. *Storming: Navigating Conflict and Tension: The storming stage is characterized by the emergence of conflicts, disagreements, and power struggles within the team. As individuals become more familiar with one another, differences in opinions, working styles, and priorities may surface, leading to tension and friction. Psychological factors such as ego clashes, communication breakdowns, and perceptual biases contribute to the challenges encountered during this stage. Effective team leaders recognize the importance of addressing conflicts constructively, promoting open dialogue, and fostering a culture of respect and collaboration. By facilitating discussions, mediating disputes, and encouraging compromise, leaders can guide the team through this turbulent phase toward resolution and alignment.*

3. *Norming: Establishing Cohesion and Collaboration: During the norming stage, the team begins to establish norms, roles, and processes that govern its functioning. Individuals develop a sense of belonging and cohesion as they align their efforts toward common objectives. Psychological factors such as social conformity, group cohesion, and shared identity contribute to the development of trust and mutual respect among team members. Team leaders play a pivotal role in reinforcing positive behaviors, recognizing*

contributions, and promoting a supportive team culture. By fostering open communication, celebrating achievements, and reinforcing shared values, leaders can solidify the team's identity and promote a sense of unity and purpose.

4. *Performing: Achieving Peak Productivity: In the performing stage, the team reaches its peak productivity and effectiveness. With roles and responsibilities clearly defined, and conflicts resolved, team members collaborate seamlessly to achieve shared goals. Psychological factors such as intrinsic motivation, group synergy, and collective efficacy drive performance and innovation within the team. Effective team leaders provide support, guidance, and resources to empower team members to excel in their roles. By promoting autonomy, fostering a culture of continuous improvement, and celebrating successes, leaders can sustain momentum and ensure the team remains focused and motivated to deliver exceptional results.*

Understanding the psychological dynamics of team formation is essential for guiding teams through the stages of development and maximizing their potential. By recognizing the challenges and opportunities inherent in each stage, team leaders can foster a culture of collaboration, trust, and accountability that enables teams to thrive and achieve success.

Leadership in Teams: Navigating the Path to Success

Leadership plays a pivotal role in shaping the effectiveness and dynamics of teams. Effective leaders guide, inspire, and empower their teams to achieve shared goals, navigate challenges, and capitalize on opportunities. The choice of leadership style significantly influences team dynamics, communication patterns, and ultimately, performance.

1. *Transformational Leadership: Inspiring Vision and Empowerment: Transformational leaders inspire and motivate their teams by articulating a compelling vision, fostering a sense of purpose, and empowering individuals to reach their full potential. They lead by example, demonstrating passion, integrity, and commitment to the team's goals. Transformational leadership promotes open communication, collaboration, and innovation within the team, leading to higher levels of engagement and satisfaction among team members. By providing support, encouragement, and opportunities for growth, transformational leaders cultivate a culture of trust and accountability that drives team effectiveness.*

2. *Transactional Leadership: Clarifying Expectations and Accountability: Transactional leaders focus on establishing clear expectations, roles, and rewards within the team. They*

use contingent rewards and corrective feedback to motivate team members and ensure adherence to established standards and procedures. Transactional leadership promotes efficiency, consistency, and performance through structured processes and systems. However, it may also stifle creativity and initiative by emphasizing compliance over empowerment. Effective transactional leaders strike a balance between maintaining stability and promoting innovation within the team, leveraging rewards and recognition to reinforce desired behaviors and outcomes.

3. *Servant Leadership: Fostering Support and Empathy: Servant leaders prioritize the well-being and development of their team members above their own interests. They demonstrate humility, empathy, and a genuine concern for the needs and aspirations of others. Servant leadership promotes a culture of collaboration, trust, and mutual respect, where team members feel valued and supported in their endeavors. By removing obstacles, facilitating growth opportunities, and advocating for their team's interests, servant leaders empower individuals to contribute their best and achieve collective success. Servant leadership fosters strong interpersonal relationships and a sense of community within the team, leading to higher levels of satisfaction and engagement.*

4. *Situational Leadership: Adapting to Context and Needs: Situational leaders adjust their leadership style based on the specific needs and circumstances of the team. They recognize that different situations may require varying degrees of direction, support, and autonomy. Situational leadership promotes flexibility, responsiveness, and adaptability in leadership approaches, enabling leaders to effectively address the evolving challenges and opportunities facing the team. By assessing the readiness and capabilities of team members, situational leaders provide tailored guidance and support to facilitate their development and success. This adaptive approach fosters trust, collaboration, and resilience within the team, enhancing its ability to navigate complex situations and achieve desired outcomes.*

Leadership plays a critical role in shaping the effectiveness and dynamics of teams. Different leadership styles offer unique approaches to motivating, guiding, and empowering team members. By understanding the strengths and limitations of each style and adapting their approach to fit the needs of the team, leaders can foster a culture of collaboration, innovation, and high performance that drives organizational success.

Strategies for Improving Communication within Teams

- *Establish Clear Channels: Define clear communication channels and protocols within the team to ensure that information flows smoothly and efficiently. This may include regular team meetings, email updates, and project management tools that facilitate collaboration and information sharing.*

- *Foster Active Listening: Encourage active listening among team members by practicing empathy, asking clarifying questions, and paraphrasing to ensure understanding. Active listening promotes mutual respect and understanding, leading to more meaningful and productive interactions within the team.*

- *Promote Open Dialogue: Create a culture of openness and transparency where team members feel comfortable expressing their thoughts, concerns, and ideas. Encourage constructive feedback and dissent, as differing perspectives can lead to more innovative solutions and better decision-making.*

- *Clarify Expectations: Clearly communicate roles, responsibilities, and expectations to ensure that everyone understands their role in achieving team goals. Establish clear objectives, deadlines, and performance metrics to provide a framework for accountability and success.*

- *Use Visual Aids: Visual aids such as charts, diagrams, and presentations can help convey complex information and ideas more effectively. Visual communication enhances understanding and retention, particularly for visual learners, and can facilitate more engaging and interactive discussions within the team.*

- *Embrace Technology: Leverage technology tools and platforms to facilitate communication and collaboration among team members, especially in remote or distributed teams. Utilize video conferencing, instant messaging, and project management software to stay connected and informed in real-time.*

- *Provide Feedback: Offer regular feedback and recognition to team members to reinforce positive behaviors and promote continuous improvement. Constructive feedback helps individuals identify areas for growth and development, while positive reinforcement boosts morale and motivation within the team.*

- *Resolve Conflicts Promptly: Address conflicts and disagreements promptly and constructively to prevent them from escalating and undermining team effectiveness. Encourage open dialogue, active listening, and compromise to find mutually acceptable solutions that preserve relationships and promote team cohesion.*

By implementing these strategies, teams can enhance their communication effectiveness and create a collaborative and supportive environment where individuals can thrive and contribute their best towards achieving shared goals. Effective communication fosters trust, engagement, and innovation, positioning teams for success in today's dynamic and competitive business landscape.

Conflict Resolution in Teams: Navigating Differences Toward Collaboration

Conflicts are an inevitable aspect of team dynamics, arising from differences in perspectives, priorities, and personalities among team members. While conflicts may disrupt team cohesion and productivity, effectively resolving them can lead to greater understanding, innovation, and growth. By understanding the root causes of conflicts and implementing strategies for resolution, teams can transform discord into opportunities for collaboration and collective success.

1. Common Causes of Conflict in Teams

a. Differences in Goals and Priorities: Conflicts often arise when team members have conflicting goals, priorities, or interests. Misalignment in objectives can lead to competition for resources, recognition, or influence within the team.

b. Communication Breakdowns: Poor communication, misunderstandings, and misinterpretations can lead to conflicts within teams. Ambiguity, lack of clarity, and ineffective communication channels can exacerbate tensions and foster resentment among team members.

c. Personality Clashes: Differences in personalities, working styles, and communication preferences can lead to interpersonal conflicts within teams. Ego clashes, misunderstandings, and perceived slights can escalate tensions and disrupt team dynamics.

d. Role Ambiguity and Overlap: Unclear roles, responsibilities, and authority can lead to conflicts within teams. Ambiguity about who is responsible for what tasks, decision-making, or accountability can create confusion and resentment among team members.

2. Strategies for Resolving Conflicts in Teams:

a. Foster Open Dialogue: Encourage open and honest communication among team members to address conflicts constructively. Create a safe and respectful environment where individuals feel comfortable expressing their concerns, opinions, and perspectives.

b. Practice Active Listening: Foster empathy and understanding by practicing active listening during conflict resolution discussions. Encourage team members to listen attentively, ask clarifying questions, and paraphrase to ensure mutual understanding.

c. Identify Common Goals: Focus on shared goals and interests to find common ground and foster collaboration. Encourage team members to identify shared objectives and brainstorm mutually beneficial solutions that address underlying concerns.

d. Collaborative Problem-Solving: Adopt a collaborative problem-solving approach that involves all relevant stakeholders in the resolution process. Encourage creativity, flexibility, and compromise to explore alternative solutions and reach win-win outcomes.

e. Clarify Roles and Expectations: Address role ambiguity and overlap by clarifying roles, responsibilities, and expectations within the team. Establish clear guidelines, processes, and communication channels to prevent misunderstandings and conflicts.

f. Seek Mediation: In cases where conflicts persist or escalate, consider seeking external mediation or facilitation to facilitate resolution. A neutral third party can help defuse tensions, facilitate communication, and guide the team towards mutually acceptable solutions.

g. Focus on Solutions, Not Blame: Encourage a solution-oriented mindset that focuses on finding constructive solutions rather than assigning blame or fault. Emphasize the importance of moving forward collaboratively and learning from conflicts to strengthen team relationships and performance.

h. Follow-Up and Monitor Progress: Ensure that agreements reached during conflict resolution discussions are implemented effectively and monitored over time. Follow up with team members regularly to assess progress, address any lingering issues, and reinforce positive behaviors.

By implementing these strategies, teams can effectively manage conflicts and transform them into opportunities for growth, collaboration, and improved performance. Conflict resolution fosters trust, communication, and cohesion within teams, enabling them to navigate challenges and achieve shared goals effectively.

Motivation and Team Performance: Driving Success Through Engagement

Motivation serves as the engine that drives team performance, influencing individuals' willingness to invest effort, persist in the face of challenges, and contribute to the team's goals. Several theories of motivation offer insights into the factors that influence individuals' motivation levels and how leaders can leverage these theories to enhance team performance. For instance, Maslow's Hierarchy of Needs posits that individuals are motivated by a hierarchy of needs, ranging from basic physiological needs to higher-order needs such as self-actualization. In a team setting, leaders can support team members' motivation by ensuring that their basic needs, such as safety, belongingness, and esteem, are met through a supportive work environment, opportunities for social connection, and recognition for their contributions. Additionally, Herzberg's Two-Factor Theory suggests that job satisfaction and motivation are influenced by two sets of factors: hygiene factors, which relate to the work environment and extrinsic motivators, and motivators, which relate to the nature of the work itself and intrinsic motivators. Leaders can enhance team motivation by providing meaningful work, opportunities for growth and development, and recognition for achievements, thereby fostering a sense of fulfillment and engagement among team members.

Leaders play a crucial role in motivating team members and enhancing team performance through various strategies. Firstly, leaders can set clear and challenging goals that inspire and motivate team members to strive for excellence. By articulating a compelling vision and aligning team goals with organizational objectives, leaders provide a sense of purpose and direction that energizes and focuses the team. Secondly, leaders can empower team members by delegating authority and decision-making responsibilities, thereby fostering autonomy, ownership, and accountability within the team. Empowered team members are more likely to take initiative, innovate, and perform at their best, leading to improved team performance. Additionally, leaders can cultivate a positive and supportive team culture that celebrates diversity, encourages collaboration, and values open communication and feedback. By fostering a culture of trust, respect, and psychological safety, leaders create an environment where team members feel valued, respected, and motivated to contribute their best, ultimately driving team performance and success.

Team Decision Making: Navigating Complexity Toward Effective Outcomes

Team decision-making processes involve the collective effort of team members to analyze information, evaluate options, and reach consensus on the best course of action. Various factors can influence the quality of these decisions, ranging from group dynamics and communication patterns to individual biases and decision-making styles.

1.

Group Dynamics and Communication Patterns: Group dynamics play a significant role in shaping team decision-making processes. Factors such as group cohesion, leadership style, and communication patterns can impact how information is shared, debated, and integrated into the decision-making process. Effective communication channels, open dialogue, and active listening promote the exchange of diverse perspectives and ideas, leading to more informed and robust decisions. Conversely, communication breakdowns, dominance by certain team members, or conformity pressures can hinder critical thinking and lead to suboptimal decisions.

2.

Individual Biases and Decision-Making Styles: Individual biases and decision-making styles can influence how team members process information and evaluate options. Cognitive biases, such as confirmation bias, anchoring bias, and groupthink, can distort judgment and lead to flawed decision-making outcomes. Additionally, differences in decision-making styles, such as risk aversion versus risk-taking, or intuitive versus analytical approaches, can create tensions and conflicts within the team. Awareness of these biases and styles is essential for promoting a balanced and inclusive decision-making process that considers a range of perspectives and avoids common pitfalls.

3.

Task Complexity and Time Pressure: The complexity of the task and time pressure can impact the decision-making process and outcomes. Complex tasks may require more time and effort to gather relevant information, analyze alternatives, and weigh trade-offs effectively. In contrast, time pressure may lead to rushed decisions, overlooking important details, or settling for the first available option rather than exploring alternatives comprehensively. Effective team decision making involves balancing the need for thorough analysis with the urgency of the situation, prioritizing critical tasks, and allocating resources accordingly.

4.

Leadership and Facilitation: Leadership and facilitation play a crucial role in guiding team decision-making processes and ensuring their effectiveness. A skilled leader can provide direction, structure, and support to facilitate productive discussions, manage conflicts, and steer the team toward consensus. Effective facilitation involves setting clear objectives, establishing ground rules, and managing group dynamics to promote active participation and collaboration. Additionally, leaders can leverage decision-making tools and techniques, such as brainstorming, SWOT analysis, or consensus-building exercises, to facilitate the decision-making process and enhance its outcomes.

Team decision making is a complex and multifaceted process influenced by a variety of factors. By understanding the dynamics of group interaction, recognizing individual biases, and fostering effective communication and leadership, teams can improve the quality of their decisions and achieve better outcomes. Embracing diversity, promoting open dialogue, and cultivating a culture of critical thinking and continuous improvement are essential for navigating the challenges of team decision making and driving success in today's dynamic and competitive business environment.

Diversity in Teams: Embracing Differences for Enhanced Performance

Diversity in teams brings a myriad of benefits, ranging from increased creativity and innovation to broader perspectives and better decision-making. By incorporating individuals from diverse backgrounds, cultures, and experiences, teams can draw upon a rich tapestry of ideas and insights that fuel creativity and problem-solving. Moreover, diversity fosters a culture of inclusion and belonging, where individuals feel valued for their unique perspectives and contributions. This sense of belonging promotes higher levels of engagement, commitment, and satisfaction among team members, leading to improved morale and productivity. Additionally, diverse teams are better equipped to anticipate and adapt to changing market dynamics, as they can tap into a wider range of customer preferences and cultural nuances, leading to more effective and responsive strategies.

However, diversity in teams also presents challenges that must be effectively managed to reap its full benefits. Differences in communication styles, working preferences, and cultural norms can lead to misunderstandings, conflicts, and friction within the team. Moreover, unconscious biases and stereotypes may impact how individuals perceive and interact with one another, undermining trust and collaboration. To address these challenges, teams must prioritize inclusive leadership, foster open dialogue, and promote cultural competence and empathy among team members. By embracing diversity as a source of strength rather than a source of division, teams can leverage their differences to foster creativity, resilience, and innovation, ultimately driving improved team effectiveness and organizational success.

Assessing Team Performance: Metrics and Strategies for Success

Assessing team performance is essential for identifying strengths, areas for improvement, and opportunities for growth. Various methods can be utilized to evaluate team performance, including objective metrics, qualitative feedback, and self-assessment tools. Objective metrics such as key performance indicators (KPIs), productivity metrics, and project milestones provide tangible measures of team performance and progress toward goals. Additionally, qualitative feedback from stakeholders, clients, and team members can offer valuable insights into the team's effectiveness, communication dynamics, and collaboration. Self-assessment tools, such as surveys or assessments, allow team members to reflect on their performance, identify strengths and weaknesses, and set goals for improvement. By utilizing a combination of these methods, teams can gain a comprehensive understanding of their performance and take targeted actions to enhance effectiveness.

Strategies for improving team performance encompass a range of approaches aimed at optimizing team dynamics, communication processes, and collaboration. Firstly, fostering a culture of continuous improvement and learning encourages team members to seek feedback, share best practices, and adapt to changing circumstances. Secondly, providing opportunities for skills development and training enables team members to acquire new competencies and enhance their capabilities. Thirdly, promoting accountability and ownership empowers team members to take ownership of their roles, responsibilities, and contributions to the team's success. Additionally, fostering a supportive and inclusive team culture, where diverse perspectives are valued and respected, promotes trust, cohesion, and collaboration. By implementing these strategies, teams can unleash their full potential, achieve greater synergy, and drive sustained success.

Questions:

1. *What are the key stages of team formation according to Tuckman's model (forming, storming, norming, performing, adjourning), and how can leaders effectively guide their teams through each stage to enhance performance and cohesiveness?*

2. *How can leaders foster diversity within their teams, and what are the potential benefits and challenges of having a diverse team in terms of creativity, decision-making, and problem-solving?*

3. *Discuss the strategies that leaders can use to build and maintain group cohesiveness. How does cohesiveness impact team performance and member satisfaction?*

4. *What role does effective communication play in building and leading high-performing teams? Provide examples of communication practices that can enhance team collaboration and trust.*

5. *How can leaders identify and leverage the individual strengths and skills of team members to optimize team performance? Discuss the importance of role clarity and task allocation in achieving team goals.*

CHAPTER NINE

Managing Diversity and Inclusion

"Strength lies in differences, not in similarities." - Stephen R. Covey

This quote by Stephen R. Covey highlights the idea that the true power and potential of any group or organization come from embracing and leveraging its diversity. When we bring together individuals with varied backgrounds, perspectives, and experiences, we create a richer tapestry of ideas and solutions. Diversity fosters creativity and innovation because it allows for a multitude of viewpoints, leading to more comprehensive and effective problem-solving. In contrast, homogeneity can lead to groupthink, where the lack of differing opinions stifles creativity and progress. By valuing and integrating differences, we build stronger, more adaptable, and more resilient teams and communities.

Diversity, equity, and inclusion (DEI) are three interrelated concepts crucial for fostering a healthy and productive organizational environment.

Diversity: *Diversity refers to the presence of a wide range of human qualities and attributes within a group, organization, or community. This includes but is not limited to differences in race, ethnicity, gender, sexual orientation, age, socio-economic status, religion, physical ability, and more. In an organizational context, diversity recognizes and values these differences, understanding that they contribute to a richer and more dynamic workforce. Diversity is not just about representation but also about embracing and leveraging the unique perspectives, experiences, and talents that individuals from diverse backgrounds bring to the table.*

Equity: *Equity involves ensuring fairness and impartiality in processes, procedures, and distribution of resources within an organization. It acknowledges that individuals may start from different positions and face various barriers and challenges due to systemic inequalities. Equity seeks to level the playing field by providing necessary support and opportunities to address these disparities. This may involve implementing policies and practices that actively counteract discrimination and bias, such as fair hiring practices, equitable promotion opportunities, and access to resources like training and mentorship. Equity aims for equality of outcome, not just equality of opportunity, recognizing and addressing historical and* *systemic disadvantages.*

Inclusion: *Inclusion refers to creating an environment where all individuals feel valued, respected, and supported, regardless of their differences. It involves fostering a sense of belonging and ensuring that every person's voice is heard and considered. Inclusion goes beyond mere tolerance or diversity metrics; it requires actively promoting participation, collaboration, and engagement from all members of the organization. Inclusive organizations strive to create spaces where diverse perspectives are welcomed, where individuals can bring their authentic selves to work without fear of discrimination or prejudice. Inclusion is essential for unlocking the full potential of a diverse workforce, driving innovation, creativity, and organizational effectiveness.*

DEI is significant for several reasons:

- *Improved Performance: Research has consistently shown that diverse teams outperform homogeneous ones. By embracing diversity, organizations can access a wider range of perspectives and ideas, leading to more innovative solutions, better decision-making, and increased creativity.*
- *Enhanced Reputation and Brand Image: In today's socially conscious world, consumers, investors, and employees increasingly expect organizations to demonstrate a commitment to DEI. Companies that prioritize diversity, equity, and inclusion not only attract top talent but also build stronger relationships with customers and stakeholders.*
- *Mitigation of Legal and Reputational Risks: Failure to address issues of discrimination, inequality, or exclusion can lead to legal liabilities, damage to reputation, and loss of trust from employees and the public. Proactively promoting DEI helps mitigate these risks and demonstrates organizational integrity.*
- *Employee Engagement and Retention: A diverse and inclusive workplace fosters a sense of belonging and loyalty among employees. When individuals feel valued and respected, they are more likely to be engaged, productive, and committed to their organization. This, in turn, reduces turnover and associated recruitment costs.*
- *Innovation and Problem-Solving: Different perspectives and experiences can lead to more robust problem-solving and innovative solutions. Organizations that embrace DEI create environments where individuals feel empowered to contribute their unique insights, leading to more effective responses to complex challenges.*

Overall, diversity, equity, and inclusion are not just moral imperatives but also strategic priorities for organizations seeking to thrive in today's diverse and rapidly changing world. By fostering environments where all individuals can contribute and succeed, organizations can unlock the full potential of their workforce and drive sustainable growth and success.

In today's globalized and interconnected world, managing diversity and inclusion has become a critical aspect of organizational success and societal progress. Diversity encompasses a wide range of differences among people, including race, ethnicity, gender, age, religion, disability, sexual orientation, socioeconomic background, and more. Inclusion, on the other hand, refers to creating an environment where all individuals feel valued, respected, and empowered to contribute their unique perspectives and talents. Effective diversity and inclusion management not only enhances organizational performance and innovation but also promotes social equity and cohesion.

Emerging examples from various sectors highlight the importance and benefits of embracing diversity and inclusion. For instance, in the tech industry, companies like Google and Microsoft have implemented comprehensive diversity and inclusion programs to address gender and racial imbalances. These initiatives include mentorship programs, diversity training, and inclusive hiring practices aimed at fostering a more diverse workforce and inclusive workplace culture. As a result, these companies have seen improvements in creativity, problem-solving, and employee satisfaction.

In the realm of education, universities such as Harvard and Stanford are leading efforts to diversify their student and faculty populations. They are implementing policies to recruit students from underrepresented backgrounds and creating inclusive curricula that reflect diverse perspectives. These efforts not only enrich the educational experience for all students but also prepare them to thrive in a diverse world.

In the public sector, governments are recognizing the value of diversity and inclusion in policymaking and public service. For example, the Canadian government has introduced policies to promote gender equality and indigenous representation within its workforce. These policies ensure that diverse voices are heard in decision-making processes, leading to more equitable and effective governance.

These emerging examples demonstrate that managing diversity and inclusion is not just a moral imperative but also a strategic advantage. Organizations and institutions that prioritize diversity and inclusion are better positioned to attract top talent, innovate, and meet the needs of a diverse customer base. As we move forward, the commitment to diversity and inclusion will be essential in building more equitable, dynamic, and resilient societies.

Understanding Diversity in the Workplace

In today's globalized and interconnected world, diversity in the workplace is not just a buzzword but a fundamental aspect of organizational culture and success. Diversity encompasses a wide range of differences among individuals, including but not limited to race, ethnicity, gender, age, sexual orientation, religion, disability, socioeconomic background, and cultural heritage. It goes beyond mere representation to encompass the full spectrum of human experiences, perspectives, and identities. Understanding and embracing diversity in the workplace is essential for fostering creativity, innovation, and inclusivity, as well as for driving organizational performance and growth.

The Value of Diversity

Diversity in the workplace brings a multitude of benefits to organizations and teams. Firstly, it fosters creativity and innovation by bringing together individuals with diverse backgrounds, perspectives, and skills. When people from different walks of life come together, they bring unique insights and approaches to problem-solving, leading to more innovative solutions and products. Additionally, diversity enhances decision-making processes by promoting critical thinking and avoiding groupthink. When teams consist of individuals with varied viewpoints, they are more likely to consider a wider range of options and make better-informed decisions.

Furthermore, diversity enhances employee engagement and satisfaction by creating a sense of belonging and inclusion. When employees feel valued and respected for who they are, they are more motivated to contribute their best work and are more likely to stay with the organization long-term. Diversity also improves customer relations and market reach by enabling organizations to better understand and serve diverse customer segments. A diverse workforce reflects the diversity of the customer base, leading to more effective communication, product development, and marketing strategies.

Challenges and Barriers

While diversity offers numerous benefits, it also presents challenges and barriers that must be addressed. One of the main challenges is unconscious bias, which refers to the implicit preferences or stereotypes that influence our perceptions and decision-making processes. Unconscious bias can lead to discrimination, exclusion, and unequal treatment of certain groups within the organization. It is essential for organizations to raise awareness about unconscious bias and implement strategies to mitigate its impact, such as bias training, diverse hiring practices, and inclusive leadership development.

Another challenge is the lack of representation and inclusion of marginalized groups, particularly in leadership positions. Despite progress in recent years, many organizations still struggle to achieve gender and racial diversity at the highest levels. This lack of representation not only perpetuates inequality but also hinders organizational performance and innovation. Organizations must work proactively to remove barriers to advancement for underrepresented groups and create pathways for diverse talent to succeed and thrive.

Creating a Culture of Inclusion

Creating a culture of inclusion is essential for harnessing the benefits of diversity in the workplace. Inclusive organizations value and celebrate differences, treat all employees with respect and dignity, and provide equal opportunities for growth and development. They foster open communication, collaboration, and teamwork, where every voice is heard and valued. Inclusive organizations also cultivate a sense of belonging and psychological safety, where employees feel comfortable being their authentic selves and expressing their ideas and opinions without fear of judgment or reprisal.

To foster a culture of inclusion, organizations must take a holistic approach that encompasses leadership commitment, policy and practice, and employee engagement. Leaders must lead by example and demonstrate their commitment to diversity and inclusion through their actions and behaviors. They must champion diversity initiatives, hold themselves and others accountable for inclusive behaviors, and create opportunities for diverse voices to be heard and represented. Policies and practices must be reviewed and updated to remove biases and barriers and promote diversity and inclusion at all levels of the organization. Finally, employees must be engaged and empowered to participate in diversity and inclusion efforts through training, education, and resource groups.

Understanding and embracing diversity in the workplace is essential for creating a culture of inclusivity, innovation, and success. Diversity brings a multitude of benefits to organizations, including increased creativity, better decision-making, and improved employee engagement and satisfaction. However, achieving diversity and inclusion requires proactive effort and commitment from leaders, employees, and organizations as a whole. By valuing and celebrating differences, addressing unconscious bias and barriers, and fostering a culture of inclusion, organizations can harness the full potential of their diverse workforce and drive sustainable growth and success in the global marketplace.

The Benefits of an Inclusive Environment

In today's dynamic and interconnected world, businesses and organizations are constantly seeking new ways to thrive in an increasingly competitive landscape. One strategy that has emerged as a key driver of success is the cultivation of an inclusive environment. An inclusive environment is one where every individual feels valued, respected, and empowered to contribute their unique perspectives and talents. Beyond being simply the right thing to do, fostering inclusivity within an organization brings a myriad of benefits that directly contribute to its success and sustainability.

Fostering Creativity and Innovation

One of the most significant benefits of an inclusive environment is its ability to foster creativity and innovation. When individuals from diverse backgrounds, experiences, and perspectives come together, they bring a wealth of ideas and approaches to problem-solving. In an inclusive environment, all voices are heard and respected, leading to a culture of collaboration and idea-sharing. This diversity of thought sparks creativity and innovation, as team members are encouraged to think outside the box and explore new possibilities. By leveraging the full spectrum of human experiences, organizations can develop groundbreaking products, services, and solutions that set them apart from the competition.

Driving Employee Engagement and Satisfaction

An inclusive environment also has a profound impact on employee engagement and satisfaction. When individuals feel valued and respected for who they are, they are more motivated to give their best effort and fully engage in their work. Inclusive organizations prioritize transparency, fairness, and open communication, creating a sense of trust and belonging among employees. This leads to higher levels of job satisfaction, retention, and loyalty. Employees who feel included are also more likely to collaborate effectively with their colleagues, resulting in increased productivity and performance across the organization.

Enhancing Decision-Making and Problem-Solving

Inclusive environments promote better decision-making and problem-solving by incorporating diverse viewpoints and perspectives into the process. When teams consist of individuals with varied backgrounds and experiences, they are more equipped to consider a wide range of options and anticipate potential challenges. Inclusive organizations encourage constructive debate and dialogue, challenging assumptions and biases that may otherwise go unexamined. This results in more robust and well-informed decisions that reflect the needs and interests of all stakeholders. By embracing diversity of thought, organizations can navigate complex issues more effectively and adapt to changing market dynamics with agility and resilience.

Cultivating a Positive Organizational Culture

Finally, an inclusive environment contributes to the cultivation of a positive organizational culture characterized by trust, respect, and mutual support. Inclusive organizations prioritize fairness and equity in all aspects of their operations, from hiring and promotion to compensation and recognition. They actively work to remove barriers to advancement for underrepresented groups and create opportunities for all employees to succeed and thrive. This commitment to inclusivity fosters a sense of pride and belonging among employees, leading to a stronger sense of community and camaraderie. In turn, this positive culture attracts top talent, enhances employer brand reputation, and strengthens the organization's position as an employer of choice.

The benefits of an inclusive environment extend far beyond mere compliance or moral obligation. By fostering creativity and innovation, driving employee engagement and satisfaction, enhancing decision-making and problem-solving, and cultivating a positive organizational culture, inclusivity directly contributes to an organization's success and sustainability. In today's rapidly evolving business landscape, organizations that prioritize inclusivity are better positioned to adapt, innovate, and thrive in an increasingly diverse and interconnected world. As we look to the future, embracing inclusivity isn't just a strategic advantage—it's a fundamental imperative for long-term success.

Strategies for Promoting Diversity and Inclusion

In an increasingly interconnected and diverse world, fostering diversity and inclusion has become not only a moral imperative but also a strategic necessity for organizations seeking to thrive in today's competitive landscape. Promoting diversity and inclusion requires a proactive and multifaceted approach that addresses barriers and biases while creating a culture where all individuals feel valued, respected, and empowered to contribute their unique perspectives and talents. Here are some key strategies for organizations to promote diversity and inclusion effectively:

1. Leadership Commitment and Accountability

Leadership commitment is essential for driving diversity and inclusion initiatives within an organization. Leaders must articulate a clear vision for diversity and inclusion and actively champion these efforts throughout the organization. They should lead by example, demonstrating inclusive behaviors and holding themselves and others accountable for fostering diversity and inclusion. This commitment should be reflected in organizational policies, practices, and decision-making processes, with diversity and inclusion metrics incorporated into performance evaluations and accountability structures.

2. Education and Training

Education and training are critical components of promoting diversity and inclusion within an organization. Employees at all levels should receive comprehensive training on topics such as unconscious bias, cultural competence, inclusive leadership, and bystander intervention.

These programs raise awareness about the impact of bias and discrimination and provide employees with the knowledge and skills to challenge stereotypes, foster inclusivity, and create a more equitable workplace. Ongoing education and training ensure that diversity and inclusion remain top priorities and are integrated into the organization's culture and operations.

3. Diverse Hiring and Recruitment Practices

Creating a diverse workforce starts with inclusive hiring and recruitment practices. Organizations should implement strategies to attract and retain diverse talent, including targeted outreach efforts, partnerships with diverse communities and organizations, and inclusive job descriptions and hiring criteria. Hiring panels should be diverse and trained to recognize and mitigate bias in the selection process. Additionally, organizations should prioritize diversity and inclusion in talent development and succession planning to ensure that all employees have opportunities for growth and advancement.

4. Inclusive Workplace Policies and Practices

Organizations should review and update their policies and practices to ensure they are inclusive and equitable for all employees. This includes policies related to recruitment, hiring, promotion, compensation, benefits, and workplace accommodations. Organizations should also implement flexible work arrangements and support programs to accommodate employees with diverse needs and responsibilities. Inclusive workplace practices promote work-life balance, employee well-being, and productivity, contributing to a positive organizational culture where all employees can thrive.

5. Employee Resource Groups and Mentorship Programs

Employee resource groups (ERGs) and mentorship programs are valuable tools for promoting diversity and inclusion within an organization. ERGs provide a forum for employees with shared identities or interests to connect, support one another, and advocate for inclusion in the workplace. These groups offer networking opportunities, professional development resources, and avenues for feedback and collaboration with organizational leadership. Mentorship programs pair employees from underrepresented groups with senior leaders or peers who can provide guidance, support, and advocacy as they navigate their careers within the organization.

6. Measurement and Evaluation

Measurement and evaluation are essential for tracking progress and holding organizations accountable for their diversity and inclusion efforts. Organizations should collect and analyze data on workforce demographics, employee perceptions, and diversity-related outcomes to identify areas of strength and opportunities for improvement. Regular diversity audits and climate surveys provide valuable insights into the effectiveness of diversity and inclusion initiatives and inform future strategic planning and decision-making. By setting clear goals, measuring progress, and transparently communicating results, organizations demonstrate their commitment to diversity and inclusion and drive continuous improvement in this area.

Promoting diversity and inclusion is not just a moral imperative but a strategic imperative for organizations seeking to thrive in today's diverse and interconnected world. By implementing proactive strategies that address barriers and biases, foster leadership commitment and accountability, provide education and training, prioritize diverse hiring and recruitment, implement inclusive workplace policies and practices, and support employee resource groups and mentorship programs, organizations can create a culture where all individuals feel valued, respected, and empowered to contribute their unique perspectives and talents. In doing so, they not only enhance their organizational performance and competitiveness but also contribute to a more equitable and inclusive society.

Inclusion in Organizations: Building a Culture of Belonging and Equity

In today's diverse and interconnected world, fostering inclusion within organizations has become a crucial aspect of building a thriving and sustainable workplace culture. Inclusion goes beyond mere representation or diversity; it's about creating an environment where every individual feels valued, respected, and empowered to contribute their unique perspectives and talents. From the boardroom to the breakroom, cultivating a culture of inclusion is essential for unlocking the full potential of employees, driving innovation, and promoting organizational success.

Embracing Diversity

At the heart of inclusion lies the recognition and celebration of diversity. Organizations are comprised of individuals from various backgrounds, experiences, and identities, each bringing their own set of strengths, ideas, and viewpoints to the table. Embracing diversity means acknowledging and appreciating these differences, rather than seeking conformity or homogeneity. It means creating space for individuals to be their authentic selves, without fear of judgment or discrimination. By embracing diversity, organizations can tap into a wealth of perspectives and insights, leading to more creative problem-solving and innovative solutions.

Fostering a Sense of Belonging

Inclusive organizations prioritize fostering a sense of belonging among all employees. Belonging is about feeling accepted, valued, and respected for who you are, regardless of your background or identity. It's about creating an environment where every individual feels like they are an integral part of the team, where their contributions are recognized and appreciated. Organizations can foster belonging by promoting open communication, collaboration, and mutual respect among employees. By creating a culture of belonging, organizations can enhance employee engagement, satisfaction, and retention, leading to a more productive and cohesive workforce.

Removing Barriers and Bias

Inclusive organizations are committed to removing barriers and bias that may hinder the full participation and advancement of all employees. This includes addressing systemic inequalities, unconscious bias, and microaggressions that may occur within the workplace. It means creating equitable policies and practices that promote fairness and opportunity for all employees, regardless of their background or identity. Organizations can implement strategies such as bias training, inclusive hiring practices, and diversity and inclusion task forces to address these issues proactively. By removing barriers and bias, organizations can create a level playing field where every individual has the opportunity to succeed and thrive.

Promoting Inclusive Leadership

Leadership plays a critical role in fostering inclusion within organizations. Inclusive leaders lead by example, demonstrating empathy, authenticity, and humility in their interactions with employees. They actively seek out diverse perspectives and input, and they empower employees to voice their opinions and ideas. Inclusive leaders prioritize fairness and transparency in their decision-making processes, and they hold themselves and others accountable for fostering a culture of inclusion. By promoting inclusive leadership, organizations can create a culture where diversity is celebrated, and every individual feels valued and respected.

Inclusion is not just a buzzword or a checkbox to be ticked—it's a fundamental aspect of building a thriving and sustainable workplace culture. By embracing diversity, fostering a sense of belonging, removing barriers and bias, and promoting inclusive leadership, organizations can create an environment where every individual feels valued, respected, and empowered to contribute their unique talents and perspectives. In doing so, they not only enhance employee engagement, satisfaction, and retention but also drive innovation, creativity, and organizational success in today's diverse and dynamic world.

Empowering Diversity, Equity, and Inclusion

In today's rapidly evolving global landscape, organizations are increasingly recognizing the importance of fostering diversity, equity, and inclusion (DEI) within their ranks. Beyond being a moral imperative, DEI is now widely acknowledged as a strategic imperative that drives innovation, enhances employee engagement, and fosters sustainable growth. From multinational corporations to small startups, organizations around the world are stepping up to the challenge of creating more diverse, equitable, and inclusive workplaces. Here, we explore some of the key contributions, initiatives, and best practices that organizations are implementing to advance DEI.

1. Leadership Commitment and Accountability

One of the most crucial contributions to DEI within organizations comes from top leadership. When leaders commit to and prioritize DEI initiatives, it sends a clear message throughout the organization that diversity and inclusion are not just buzzwords but fundamental values. Leaders must lead by example, demonstrating their commitment to DEI through their actions, behaviors, and decision-making processes. They should hold themselves and others accountable for fostering a culture of inclusivity and equity, with DEI metrics integrated into performance evaluations and strategic planning processes.

2. Diversity Recruitment and Hiring Practices

Another key initiative in promoting DEI within organizations is the adoption of diverse recruitment and hiring practices. This includes implementing strategies to attract and retain diverse talent, such as targeted outreach efforts, partnerships with diverse communities and organizations, and inclusive job descriptions and hiring criteria. Hiring panels should be diverse and trained to recognize and mitigate bias in the selection process. Additionally, organizations should prioritize diversity and inclusion in talent development and succession planning to ensure that all employees have opportunities for growth and advancement.

3. Inclusive Workplace Policies and Practices

Creating an inclusive workplace starts with reviewing and updating organizational policies and practices to ensure they are equitable and inclusive for all employees. This includes policies related to recruitment, hiring, promotion, compensation, benefits, and workplace accommodations. Organizations should also implement flexible work arrangements and support programs to accommodate employees with diverse needs and responsibilities. Inclusive workplace practices promote work-life balance, employee well-being, and productivity, contributing to a positive organizational culture where all employees can thrive.

4. Employee Resource Groups and Mentorship Programs

Employee resource groups (ERGs) and mentorship programs are valuable tools for promoting DEI within organizations. ERGs provide a forum for employees with shared identities or interests to connect, support one another, and advocate for inclusion in the workplace. These groups offer networking opportunities, professional development resources, and avenues for feedback and collaboration with organizational leadership. Mentorship programs pair employees from underrepresented groups with senior leaders or peers who can provide guidance, support, and advocacy as they navigate their careers within the organization.

5. Continuous Learning and Development

Continuous education and development on DEI topics are essential for fostering a culture of inclusivity within organizations. Employees at all levels should receive comprehensive training on topics such as unconscious bias, cultural competence, inclusive leadership, and bystander intervention. These programs raise awareness about the impact of bias and discrimination and provide employees with the knowledge and skills to challenge stereotypes, foster inclusivity, and create a more equitable workplace. Ongoing education and training ensure that DEI remains a top priority and is integrated into the organization's culture and operations.

Organizations play a crucial role in advancing diversity, equity, and inclusion in today's society. By committing to DEI initiatives, implementing best practices, and fostering a culture of inclusivity, organizations can create workplaces where all individuals feel valued, respected, and empowered to contribute their unique talents and perspectives. Through these collective efforts, organizations can drive innovation, enhance employee engagement, and ultimately, build a more equitable and inclusive society for all.

Questions:

1. *What are the key stages of team formation according to Tuckman's model (forming, storming, norming, performing, adjourning), and how can leaders effectively guide their teams through each stage to enhance performance and cohesiveness?*

2. *How can leaders foster diversity within their teams, and what are the potential benefits and challenges of having a diverse team in terms of creativity, decision-making, and problem-solving?*

3. *Discuss the strategies that leaders can use to build and maintain group cohesiveness. How does cohesiveness impact team performance and member satisfaction?*

4. *What role does effective communication play in building and leading high-performing teams? Provide examples of communication practices that can enhance team collaboration and trust.*

5. *How can leaders identify and leverage the individual strengths and skills of team members to optimize team performance? Discuss the importance of role clarity and task allocation in achieving team goals.*

CHAPTER TEN

Ethical Decision-Making and Corporate Social Responsibility

> *"Ethics is knowing the difference between what you have a right to do and what is right to do." — Potter Stewart*

Potter Stewart, an Associate Justice of the United States Supreme Court, highlights a fundamental distinction in ethical decision making: the difference between legal rights and moral rights. This quote emphasizes that just because an action is legally permissible does not necessarily make it ethically sound.

In the context of managerial psychology, this quote underscores the importance of leaders and managers making decisions that are not only compliant with laws and regulations but also align with higher moral standards and principles. Ethical decision making involves considering the broader impact of actions on stakeholders, including employees, customers, and the community, and striving to do what is morally right even when it may not be explicitly required by law.

This perspective encourages managers to:

- *Evaluate Consequences: Consider the outcomes of their decisions on various stakeholders.*
- *Reflect on Values: Align decisions with core ethical values such as honesty, fairness, and integrity.*
- *Seek Guidance: Use ethical frameworks and consult with others when facing complex dilemmas.*

Promote a Culture of Ethics: Foster an organizational environment where ethical behavior is valued and rewarded.

Decision-making theories explore how individuals and groups make choices and the processes they use to select among alternatives. Here are some key theories in decision making:

1. Rational Decision-Making Model

This model assumes that decision makers are fully rational and make decisions by systematically considering all available information and alternatives. The Rational Decision-Making Model is a structured and systematic approach to making choices that involves a series of logical steps designed to lead to the most optimal decision. This model operates on the assumption that decision-makers are fully rational and have access to all necessary information, allowing them to objectively evaluate all possible alternatives. The process begins with identifying and clearly defining the problem or decision to be made. Next, relevant information is gathered and analyzed to generate a comprehensive list of potential solutions. Each alternative is then assessed based on its potential outcomes, considering both the benefits and drawbacks. The decision-maker selects the option that maximizes utility or achieves the best overall outcome. After the decision is implemented, its effectiveness is monitored and evaluated, ensuring that the desired results are achieved. While this model emphasizes logical and thorough analysis, its practical application can be limited by real-world constraints such as incomplete information, time pressures, and cognitive limitations, which can make fully rational decision-making challenging.

Steps in the Rational Decision-Making Model:

- *Identify the problem.*
- *Gather information.*
- *Generate alternatives.*
- *Evaluate alternatives.*
- *Choose the best alternative.*
-

Implement the decision.

- *Monitor and evaluate the outcome.*

2. Bounded Rationality (Herbert Simon)

Herbert Simon proposed that individuals make decisions within the constraints of limited information, time, and cognitive capacity. This leads to "satisficing" – selecting an option that is good enough rather than the optimal one. Bounded Rationality, a concept introduced by Herbert Simon, challenges the notion of the fully rational decision-maker by acknowledging the limitations inherent in human decision-making processes. According to this theory, individuals are constrained by limited information, finite cognitive resources, and restricted time when making decisions. As a result, people use simplified models and heuristics to make decisions rather than seeking the optimal solution. This leads to "satisficing," a process where decision-makers settle for a solution that is good enough to meet their needs, rather than the best possible one. Simon's theory recognizes that while individuals aim to make rational choices, their decisions are bounded by these practical limitations, making it impossible to achieve perfect rationality. Bounded Rationality thus provides a more realistic framework for understanding decision-making behavior, highlighting how people navigate complex environments with imperfect information and limited computational capacities.

- *Satisficing: Settling for an Adequate Solution*

Satisficing is a decision-making strategy that involves choosing an option that meets a minimum threshold of acceptability rather than seeking the optimal solution. This concept, introduced by Herbert Simon, reflects the reality that decision-makers often face constraints such as limited information, time pressures, and cognitive limitations, which make it impractical to thoroughly evaluate all possible alternatives. Instead of striving for the best possible outcome, individuals set criteria for what constitutes an acceptable solution and stop searching once they find an option that meets these criteria.

For example, a hiring manager looking for a new employee might set a threshold for necessary qualifications and experience. Once they find a candidate who meets these requirements, they may choose to hire that person rather than continuing the search for a potentially better candidate. Satisficing is particularly useful in complex or urgent situations where the cost of searching for the optimal solution outweighs the benefits of finding it. This approach allows decision-makers to make timely and practical decisions, although it may sometimes result in suboptimal outcomes.

- *Heuristics: Mental Shortcuts in Decision Making*

Heuristics are cognitive shortcuts or rules of thumb that individuals use to simplify decision-making processes. These mental strategies enable people to make quick and efficient decisions without having to analyze all available information in detail. Heuristics are particularly useful in situations where time is limited, information is incomplete, or the decision context is complex.

Some common types of heuristics include:

Availability Heuristic: *This involves making judgments based on the ease with which relevant examples come to mind. For instance, people might overestimate the likelihood of dramatic events like airplane crashes because such incidents are more memorable and easily recalled.*

Representativeness Heuristic*: This involves assessing the probability of an event based on how similar it is to a typical case. For example, someone might judge a person to be a librarian rather than a salesperson based on their stereotypical image of a librarian, such as being introverted and bookish.*

Anchoring and Adjustment Heuristic*: This involves relying heavily on the first piece of information encountered (the "anchor") and making subsequent judgments based on that anchor. For example, if the initial price of a product is set high, any discount may seem more attractive, even if the final price is still relatively high.*

Recognition Heuristic*: This involves making decisions based on the recognition of familiar options. For instance, when choosing between two brands, a consumer might opt for the one they recognize, assuming it to be better.*

While heuristics can lead to quick and satisfactory decisions, they can also result in systematic biases and errors. Understanding heuristics helps in recognizing their influence on decision making and mitigating potential biases, thus improving decision quality in both personal and organizational contexts.

3. Prospect Theory (Daniel Kahneman and Amos Tversky)

Prospect Theory describes how people choose between probabilistic alternatives that involve risk, where the probabilities of outcomes are known. Prospect Theory, developed by Daniel Kahneman and Amos Tversky in 1979, is a psychological theory that describes how individuals make decisions between alternatives that involve risk and uncertainty. Unlike the traditional economic theory, which assumes that people are rational actors who seek to maximize utility, Prospect Theory provides a more accurate depiction of human behavior by considering psychological biases and heuristics.

Key Concepts:

- ***Loss Aversion:*** *People tend to prefer avoiding losses over acquiring equivalent gains. People are more sensitive to losses than to equivalent gains. The pain of losing is psychologically about twice as powerful as the pleasure of gaining. This leads individuals to avoid risks when considering potential gains but to take risks to avoid potential losses.*

- ***Framing Effect:*** *The way information is presented (framed) affects decisions. The way choices are presented or "framed" significantly affects decision making. For instance, people react differently to a choice presented as a gain versus a loss, even if the actual outcomes are the same.*

  For example, a surgery with a 90% survival rate is perceived more positively than one with a 10% mortality rate, despite these statistics describing the same scenario.

- ***Value Function:*** *People evaluate potential losses and gains relative to a reference point rather than absolute outcomes. The value function is concave for gains (indicating diminishing sensitivity) and convex for losses (also indicating diminishing sensitivity), but steeper for losses than for gains.*

  This means that the subjective value of gains increases at a decreasing rate, while the subjective value of losses increases at an increasing rate. A loss of $100 feels more significant than a gain of $100, illustrating loss aversion.

- *Reference Points:* People evaluate outcomes relative to a reference point rather than based on absolute outcomes. This reference point is often the status quo or the current situation. Gains and losses are determined relative to this reference point. For instance, the same $100 can be perceived as a significant gain or a minor loss depending on the reference point.

- *Probability Weighting:* People tend to overestimate the likelihood of rare events and underestimate the likelihood of moderate and high-probability events. This is known as the probability weighting function. This causes individuals to overvalue unlikely events (like winning a lottery) and undervalue more certain outcomes.

Implications of Prospect Theory:

Prospect Theory has profound implications across various fields, particularly in economics, finance, and behavioral sciences. It helps explain several observed behaviors that traditional utility theory cannot:

- **Endowment Effect:** *People place a higher value on objects they own compared to objects they do not own, due to loss aversion.*

- **Insurance:** *Individuals are more likely to buy insurance to avoid potential losses than to seek potential gains.*

- **Investment Behavior:** *Investors might hold on to losing stocks longer than is rational, hoping to avoid realizing a loss, and might sell winning stocks too quickly to realize gains.*

Applications:

Behavioral Economics: Prospect Theory has been foundational in the development of behavioral economics, a field that examines how psychological factors influence economic decision making.

-

- ***Marketing and Consumer Behavior:*** *Companies use insights from Prospect Theory to frame products and pricing strategies to make them more appealing to consumers.*

- ***Public Policy:*** *Understanding how people perceive risks and rewards helps policymakers design better interventions, such as encouraging healthy behaviors or improving compliance with regulations.*

In essence, Prospect Theory reveals that human decision making is often irrational and influenced by psychological factors, providing a richer understanding of how people assess risks and make choices.

4. Decision-Making under Uncertainty

Various models address decision making when the outcomes are uncertain:

- ***Maximin and Maximax Strategies:*** *Focus on the worst-case (maximin) or best-case (maximax) scenarios. Maximin and Maximax strategies are decision-making approaches used under conditions of uncertainty, focusing respectively on the worst-case and best-case scenarios. The Maximin strategy is a conservative approach where the decision-maker considers the worst possible outcome for each option and then chooses the option with the highest minimum payoff. This strategy is particularly useful when dealing with high levels of uncertainty or when the stakes are significant, as it aims to minimize potential losses. For instance, a business deciding on an investment might use the Maximin strategy to ensure that the worst-case financial outcome is still acceptable, thus prioritizing security over potential high rewards.*

  Conversely, the Maximax strategy takes an optimistic approach, focusing on the best possible outcome for each option and selecting the option with the highest maximum payoff. This strategy is suited for risk-takers who aim to maximize potential gains, even if it involves significant risk. For example, a startup entrepreneur might use the Maximax strategy to choose a business venture with the potential for the highest profit, despite the possible risks involved. While the Maximax strategy can lead to substantial rewards, it also carries a higher risk of failure, as it does not account for less favorable outcomes.

Both strategies reflect different risk preferences and attitudes towards uncertainty: Maximin appeals to risk-averse individuals seeking security, while Maximax attracts risk-seekers willing to gamble for higher rewards. The choice between these strategies depends on the decision-maker's risk tolerance, the context of the decision, and the potential impact of the outcomes.

- **Expected Utility Theory:** *Decisions are made by considering the expected utility of each alternative, factoring in probabilities and personal preferences for risk. Expected Utility Theory (EUT) is a foundational concept in economics and decision theory that describes how rational individuals make choices under conditions of uncertainty. According to this theory, decisions are made by evaluating the expected utility of each alternative, which involves considering both the potential outcomes and their associated probabilities, as well as the individual's personal preferences for risk.*

In Expected Utility Theory, utility represents a measure of satisfaction or value that an individual derives from a particular outcome. To make a decision, the individual assigns a utility value to each possible outcome and then calculates the expected utility for each alternative by weighting these utility values by their respective probabilities. The expected utility of an alternative is the sum of the utilities of all possible outcomes, each multiplied by the probability of that outcome occurring. The decision-maker then chooses the alternative with the highest expected utility.

For example, consider a person deciding whether to invest in a high-risk, high-reward stock or a low-risk, low-reward bond. The high-risk stock might have a 50% chance of doubling the investment (high utility) and a 50% chance of losing half of it (low utility). The low-risk bond might have a 90% chance of yielding a modest return (moderate utility) and a 10% chance of breaking even (neutral utility). By calculating the expected utility for both investments, considering the probabilities and the individual's risk tolerance, the decision-maker can determine which investment provides the highest expected utility.

Expected Utility Theory accounts for individual risk preferences through the shape of the utility function. Risk-averse individuals have a concave utility function, meaning they derive less additional utility from gains and suffer more from losses. Risk-seeking individuals have a convex utility function, meaning they gain more utility from potential high rewards and are less affected by losses. Risk-neutral individuals have a linear utility function, valuing gains and losses proportionately.

The strength of Expected Utility Theory lies in its ability to provide a structured and quantitative approach to decision making under uncertainty. It helps explain why people make different choices based on their risk preferences and the probabilistic nature of outcomes. However, it also has limitations. Real-world decisions often involve complexities that EUT does not fully capture, such as cognitive biases, emotions, and imperfect information. Despite these limitations, Expected Utility Theory remains a fundamental tool for understanding and analyzing decision-making behavior in uncertain environments.

5. Group Decision-Making Models

These theories explore how groups make decisions:

Groupthink (Irving Janis): *A phenomenon where the desire for group consensus leads to poor decision making. Groupthink, a concept developed by psychologist Irving Janis in the 1970s, describes a phenomenon in which the desire for harmony and consensus within a group leads to irrational or dysfunctional decision-making outcomes. This occurs when group members prioritize unanimity over critical evaluation of alternative ideas or viewpoints, often resulting in suboptimal decisions. The key features of groupthink include a strong inclination to conform, suppression of dissenting opinions, and an illusion of unanimity.*

Characteristics of Groupthink

- *Illusion of Invulnerability: Group members may develop an excessive optimism and take extreme risks, believing their decisions cannot fail.*
- *Collective Rationalization: The group discounts warnings and negative feedback, rationalizing decisions and ignoring potential problems.*
- *Belief in Inherent Morality: Members believe in the moral correctness of their group, which can lead them to overlook ethical or moral consequences of their decisions.*
- *Stereotyping of Out-Groups: The group creates negative stereotypes of those who oppose or challenge the group's ideas, leading to dismissal of outside opinions.*
- *Direct Pressure on Dissenters: Members who express doubts or opposing views face direct pressure to conform, leading to self-censorship.*
- *Self-Censorship: Individuals suppress their own doubts and counterarguments to avoid conflict or disapproval from the group.*
-

Illusion of Unanimity: The lack of dissent is mistaken for unanimous agreement, reinforcing the group's decisions.

- *Mindguards: Some members take on the role of protecting the group from dissenting information, further isolating the group from alternative perspectives.*

Consequences of Groupthink

Groupthink can lead to a variety of negative outcomes, including:

- *Incomplete Analysis: The group fails to consider all possible alternatives and their consequences, leading to poor decision-making.*
- *Lack of Contingency Plans: Overconfidence and a lack of critical discussion result in inadequate planning for potential problems.*
- *Poor Risk Assessment: The group's illusion of invulnerability and collective rationalization lead to underestimating risks and overestimating benefits.*
- *Ethical Lapses: The belief in the group's inherent morality can result in decisions that ignore ethical considerations.*

Examples of Groupthink

Several historical events have been attributed to groupthink:

Bay of Pigs Invasion (1961): The U.S. government's failed invasion of Cuba, where dissenting opinions within the administration were suppressed, leading to a poorly planned and executed operation.

Challenger Space Shuttle Disaster (1986): NASA's decision to launch the Challenger despite engineers' concerns about the O-rings, which led to the shuttle's explosion and the death of seven astronauts.

Watergate Scandal (1972): The Nixon administration's decision to engage in and cover up illegal activities, with advisors suppressing doubts about the ethical and legal implications.

Wells Fargo account scandal (2016): Employees of Wells Fargo, under intense pressure to meet aggressive sales targets, opened millions of unauthorized bank and credit card accounts for customers without their consent. This unethical behavior persisted for years, driven by a corporate culture that emphasized sales goals and rewarded employees for meeting targets. Despite warnings from lower-level employees and internal audits flagging irregularities, upper management chose to ignore or downplay these concerns, preferring to maintain the illusion of high performance and profitability. This collective blindness to the ethical implications of their actions, coupled with a desire to preserve the image of success, ultimately resulted in significant financial and reputational damage to the bank, leading to regulatory investigations, fines, and the resignation of top executives. The Wells Fargo scandal serves as a stark reminder of how groupthink can permeate organizational cultures, leading to harmful and unethical decision-making outcomes.

Preventing Groupthink

To mitigate the risk of groupthink, organizations and groups can adopt several strategies:

- *Encourage Open Debate: Leaders should foster an environment where all members feel safe to express their opinions and doubts.*
- *Appoint a Devil's Advocate: Designating someone to challenge assumptions and propose alternative viewpoints can help prevent consensus without critical evaluation.*
- *Break into Smaller Groups: Splitting into independent subgroups to discuss issues can lead to more diverse perspectives.*
- *Seek External Opinions: Consulting with outside experts or stakeholders can provide fresh insights and prevent insularity.*
- *Leader Neutrality: Leaders should refrain from stating their preferences early in the discussion to avoid influencing the group's decision-making process.*
-

Structured Decision-Making Processes: Implementing formal procedures for evaluating alternatives and assessing risks can ensure thorough analysis.

Groupthink remains a critical concept for understanding how groups can make flawed decisions due to social dynamics. Recognizing and addressing the symptoms of groupthink is essential for fostering effective and ethical decision-making within groups and organizations.

- **Social Decision Schemes:** *Methods by which groups combine individual preferences into a collective decision (e.g., majority rule, consensus). Social Decision Schemes encompass various methods through which groups synthesize individual preferences to reach a collective decision. These mechanisms are pivotal in shaping the decision-making processes within organizations, communities, and societies. Examples include majority rule, where decisions are made based on the preferences of the largest subset of the group; consensus, which strives for unanimous agreement among all members; and plurality voting, where the option with the highest number of votes, though not necessarily a majority, prevails. Other schemes, such as dictatorial decision-making or expert opinion, prioritize the authority or expertise of a single individual or a select few. Each scheme reflects distinct trade-offs in terms of efficiency, inclusivity, and the potential for conflict resolution. By understanding and employing these decision schemes thoughtfully, groups can navigate diverse perspectives and interests more effectively, fostering consensus and collective action.*

6. Intuitive Decision Making

This approach emphasizes the role of intuition and experience in making decisions, especially under conditions of uncertainty and time pressure.

Key Concepts:

- **Recognition-Primed Decision (RPD) Model (Gary Klein)**:

  The Recognition-Primed Decision (RPD) Model, developed by psychologist Gary Klein, provides a framework for understanding how individuals make decisions under conditions of time pressure and uncertainty. Unlike traditional decision-making models that emphasize careful analysis and comparison of alternatives, the RPD model suggests that decision makers often rely on intuitive recognition of patterns and prior experiences to quickly identify and implement solutions. Key aspects of the RPD model include the role of expertise and tacit knowledge in guiding decision making, as well as the importance of situational awareness and rapid information processing. According to the RPD model, decision makers mentally simulate potential courses of action based on their past experiences and the cues present in the current situation. They then select the option that best matches the patterns they recognize, rather than evaluating multiple alternatives systematically. This intuitive decision-making process allows individuals to make rapid and effective decisions, particularly in high-stakes and time-critical situations where there is limited time for deliberation.

One important insight from the RPD model is the concept of "pattern recognition," where individuals draw on their extensive experience and expertise to quickly identify familiar situations and appropriate responses. This highlights the importance of real-world experience and practical knowledge in decision making, suggesting that expertise develops through exposure to diverse situations rather than formal training alone. Additionally, the RPD model emphasizes the role of feedback and learning in refining decision-making skills over time. By reflecting on past experiences and outcomes, individuals can enhance their ability to recognize patterns and make better decisions in the future. Overall, the RPD model offers valuable insights into the cognitive processes underlying rapid decision making, highlighting the adaptive nature of human judgment and the value of intuition in complex and dynamic environments.

- ***Heuristics and Biases:*** *Cognitive shortcuts and the systematic biases that can arise from their use (e.g., availability heuristic, anchoring). Heuristics and biases are fundamental concepts in decision-making psychology, shedding light on the cognitive shortcuts individuals employ and the systematic errors that can result from these mental processes. Heuristics are mental shortcuts or rules of thumb that allow individuals to make quick and efficient decisions by simplifying complex information. However, these heuristics can also lead to biases, or systematic deviations from rationality, when applied inappropriately. One prominent example is the availability heuristic, where individuals assess the likelihood of an event based on how easily they can recall similar instances from memory. This can lead to overestimating the probability of events that are more memorable, such as vivid or recent events, and underestimating the likelihood of less salient events. Another common heuristic is anchoring, where individuals rely too heavily on the first piece of information encountered (the "anchor") when making judgments or estimates, even if the anchor is irrelevant or misleading. This can lead to biases in judgment and decision making, as individuals may be unduly influenced by initial information and fail to adjust their judgments accordingly. These heuristics and biases play a crucial role in shaping human decision making, impacting various domains including economics, finance, and public policy. Understanding these cognitive shortcuts and their associated biases is essential for recognizing and mitigating their influence, ultimately leading to more informed and rational decision making.*

7. Behavioral Decision Theory

This theory incorporates insights from psychology to understand deviations from rational decision making.

Key Concepts:

- **Anchoring:** *Relying too heavily on the first piece of information encountered. Anchoring: Anchoring is a cognitive bias in decision making where individuals rely disproportionately on the first piece of information they encounter when making subsequent judgments or estimates. This initial information, known as the anchor, serves as a reference point that influences subsequent evaluations, even if it is irrelevant or arbitrary. Anchors can be numerical values, such as prices or quantities, or qualitative information, such as descriptions or opinions. For example, when negotiating the price of a car, the initial asking price provided by the seller can serve as an anchor, influencing the buyer's perception of a fair price. Even if the buyer knows the market value of the car is lower, the presence of the anchor can still exert a significant influence on their final offer. Anchoring can lead to systematic errors in judgment and decision making, as individuals may fail to sufficiently adjust their estimates away from the initial anchor, resulting in biased or suboptimal decisions.*

- **Overconfidence:** *Overestimating the accuracy of one's knowledge or predictions. Overconfidence is a cognitive bias characterized by the tendency to overestimate the accuracy of one's knowledge or predictions, leading individuals to have unwarranted confidence in their abilities or judgments. This bias manifests in various domains, including decision making, problem-solving, and risk assessment. For example, individuals may overestimate their performance on tasks, such as exams or job interviews, leading them to believe they are more competent than they actually are. In investment and financial decision making, overconfidence can lead individuals to take excessive risks or make speculative investments based on unfounded beliefs in their ability to predict market movements. Overconfidence can be particularly problematic when combined with anchoring, as individuals may anchor their judgments on overly optimistic or unrealistic expectations, leading to poor decision-making outcomes.*

- **Confirmation Bias:** *Seeking out information that confirms existing beliefs and ignoring contradictory evidence. Confirmation bias is a cognitive bias where individuals tend to favor information that confirms their preexisting beliefs or hypotheses, while disregarding or downplaying contradictory evidence. This bias can be particularly pronounced within organizations, where group dynamics and organizational culture can amplify its effects. For instance, consider a marketing team launching a new product campaign. If the team is convinced that their strategy is flawless, they may selectively focus on positive market research data that supports their viewpoint, while dismissing any negative feedback or market indicators suggesting otherwise. This biased interpretation of information can lead to a tunnel-vision effect within the organization, hindering its ability to adapt and respond* *effectively to changing circumstances.*

Moreover, confirmation bias within organizations can manifest in decision-making processes, where leaders and teams may seek out opinions and evidence that align with their predetermined conclusions, while ignoring dissenting voices or alternative perspectives. This can result in suboptimal choices and missed opportunities for innovation and growth. To mitigate confirmation bias, organizations can encourage a culture of open-mindedness, critical thinking, and constructive skepticism, where diverse viewpoints are welcomed, and decisions are based on a comprehensive analysis of all available evidence, rather than selective perception. Additionally, implementing processes for peer review and independent evaluation can help counteract the influence of confirmation bias and promote more objective decision-making within organizations.

8. Naturalistic Decision Making

This approach studies how people make decisions in real-world settings, emphasizing the importance of context and experience.

Key Concepts:

- ***Contextual Factors:*** *The influence of the environment and situational factors on decision making. Contextual factors refer to the broad array of environmental and situational influences that shape decision-making processes. These factors encompass elements such as cultural norms, social dynamics, economic conditions, organizational structures, and physical surroundings. Contextual factors play a crucial role in shaping individual and collective behaviors, attitudes, and choices, often exerting a significant influence on the outcomes of decisions made within various settings. For example, a decision made in a highly competitive market environment may differ significantly from one made in a monopolistic market, reflecting the impact of contextual factors on strategic planning and risk assessment. Acknowledging and understanding these contextual influences is essential for making informed decisions that account for the complexities of real-world situations and optimizing outcomes within diverse and dynamic environments.*

- ***Expertise:*** *The role of experience and knowledge in making effective decisions. Expertise refers to the accumulation of experience, knowledge, and skills within a particular domain or field, and it plays a fundamental role in facilitating effective decision-making. Individuals with expertise in a given area are better equipped to assess information, identify patterns, anticipate potential outcomes, and evaluate alternative courses of action. This expertise is developed through years of practice, learning, and exposure to diverse situations, allowing experts to draw upon a wealth of relevant knowledge and insights* *when making decisions. For instance, a seasoned surgeon's expertise enables them to quickly diagnose complex medical conditions and determine the most appropriate treatment plan, leading to better patient outcomes. In decision-making contexts, expertise enhances the ability to make informed judgments, mitigate risks, and capitalize on opportunities, ultimately contributing to more successful outcomes across various domains and disciplines.*

These theories provide a broad understanding of the various factors and processes involved in decision making, helping to explain how decisions are made in both individual and group contexts.

Ethical Theories and Principles

Ethical theories and principles serve as essential frameworks for evaluating moral dilemmas and guiding ethical decision-making in various contexts. These theories offer distinct perspectives on what constitutes right or wrong behavior and provide principles to help individuals and organizations navigate complex ethical challenges.

One of the most prominent ethical theories is ***Utilitarianism****, which proposes that the morality of an action should be judged based on its ability to maximize overall happiness or utility for the greatest number of people. In utilitarianism, the ends justify the means, and decisions are made with the goal of achieving the greatest good for the greatest number, often considering factors such as pleasure, pain, and the distribution of resources.*

Contrastingly, ***Deontological ethics*** *prioritizes adherence to moral rules or duties regardless of the consequences. Rooted in principles such as the categorical imperative proposed by Immanuel Kant, deontologists believe in acting out of a sense of duty and respecting the inherent value and dignity of individuals. According to this theory, certain actions are inherently right or wrong, regardless of their outcomes, and individuals have a duty to act in accordance with moral principles.*

Virtue ethics*, on the other hand, focuses on the character traits or virtues that lead to ethical behavior. Developed by philosophers such as Aristotle, virtue ethics emphasizes the cultivation of virtuous qualities such as honesty, compassion, courage, and integrity. Practitioners of virtue ethics aim to develop good character and make ethical decisions guided by the pursuit of excellence and the fulfillment of one's potential as a moral agent.*

Consequentialism*, another influential ethical theory, judges the morality of an action based on its outcomes. Unlike deontology, which emphasizes adherence to moral rules, consequentialist theories prioritize the consequences or results of actions. This approach* *evaluates the ethicality of decisions by considering factors such as the amount of happiness or well-being produced, the reduction of suffering, and the promotion of desirable outcomes.*

In addition to ethical theories, various ethical principles provide further guidance for ethical decision-making. These principles include autonomy, which emphasizes respecting individuals' right to make their own decisions and choices; beneficence, which entails doing good and promoting the well-being of others; nonmaleficence, which involves avoiding harm and minimizing risks; and justice, which pertains to fairness, equity, and the distribution of benefits and burdens within society.

Ethical theories and principles play a crucial role in shaping individual and collective moral reasoning, informing ethical decision-making across diverse domains such as healthcare, business, law, and governance. By providing frameworks for ethical analysis and guidance on moral behavior, these theories and principles help individuals and organizations navigate complex ethical dilemmas and strive to act in ways that uphold fundamental values and principles of morality and justice.

Role of Ethics in Management

The role of ethics in management is paramount, serving as the moral compass that guides decision-making, shapes organizational culture, and influences stakeholder relationships. Ethical considerations are central to effective management practices, as they help ensure that decisions and actions align with principles of fairness, integrity, responsibility, and accountability.

At the core of ethical management is the recognition that businesses and organizations have broader responsibilities beyond maximizing profits. Ethical managers prioritize the well-being of all stakeholders, including employees, customers, suppliers, communities, and the environment, while also considering the long-term sustainability and reputation of the organization.

Ethical management involves fostering a culture of integrity and transparency within the organization. This includes establishing clear ethical guidelines, codes of conduct, and policies that outline expected behaviors and standards of ethical conduct for employees at all levels. By promoting ethical awareness and providing guidance on ethical decision-making, managers create an environment where employees feel empowered to act ethically and responsibly in their roles.

Furthermore, ethical management requires leaders to lead by example and demonstrate ethical behavior in their own actions and decisions. When managers uphold ethical principles and demonstrate integrity, honesty, and fairness in their interactions, they set a positive tone for the entire organization and inspire trust and confidence among employees, customers, and other stakeholders.

Ethical management also entails making ethically sound decisions, even in situations where ethical considerations may conflict with short-term financial gain or other interests. This may involve prioritizing the welfare of employees, ensuring product safety and quality, respecting the rights of stakeholders, and adhering to legal and regulatory requirements.

Moreover, ethical management extends beyond the internal operations of the organization to encompass its relationships with external stakeholders and the broader community. This includes practicing ethical sourcing and supply chain management, engaging in fair and ethical marketing and advertising practices, and contributing positively to the communities in which the organization operates.

In today's increasingly interconnected and socially conscious world, ethical management is not only a moral imperative but also a strategic advantage. Organizations that prioritize ethics in their management practices are more likely to earn the trust and loyalty of customers, attract and retain top talent, build strong relationships with stakeholders, and enhance their reputation and brand value in the long term.

Ultimately, the role of ethics in management is to ensure that organizations operate in a manner that is ethical, responsible, and sustainable, contributing to the well-being of society while also achieving their business objectives. By integrating ethical considerations into all aspects of management, organizations can create a culture of integrity, trust, and accountability that drives success and fosters long-term prosperity for all stakeholders involved.

Balancing profit and social responsibility

Balancing profit and social responsibility is a fundamental challenge facing businesses and organizations in today's global economy. While profitability is essential for sustaining operations and generating returns for shareholders, organizations also have a responsibility to consider the broader social and environmental impacts of their actions. Achieving a balance between profit and social responsibility requires careful consideration of ethical principles, stakeholder interests, and long-term sustainability goals.

At the heart of this balancing act is the recognition that businesses can no longer afford to prioritize profit at the expense of social and environmental concerns. Increasingly, consumers, investors, and regulators are holding organizations accountable for their impact on society, demanding greater transparency, accountability, and ethical behavior.

Organizations that successfully balance profit and social responsibility integrate ethical considerations into their decision-making processes and business strategies. This involves adopting responsible business practices that prioritize the well-being of employees, customers, communities, and the environment, while also delivering value to shareholders.

One approach to balancing profit and social responsibility is to embrace the concept of corporate social responsibility (CSR), which involves integrating social and environmental concerns into business operations and decision-making. CSR initiatives may include ethical sourcing and supply chain management, environmental sustainability efforts, community engagement and philanthropy, and initiatives to promote diversity, equity, and inclusion within the organization.

Another key strategy for balancing profit and social responsibility is to adopt a stakeholder-oriented approach to management. This involves identifying and engaging with all stakeholders who are affected by or have a stake in the organization's activities, including employees, customers, suppliers, investors, regulators, and communities. By considering the interests and concerns of all stakeholders, organizations can make more informed decisions that take into account the broader social and environmental implications of their actions.

Furthermore, organizations can leverage the power of innovation and technology to drive both profit and social impact. By developing innovative products and services that address societal challenges and meet the needs of underserved populations, businesses can create shared value for both shareholders and society. This approach, known as social entrepreneurship or impact investing, demonstrates that profit and social responsibility are not mutually exclusive but can be mutually reinforcing.

Ultimately, achieving a balance between profit and social responsibility requires a shift in mindset and culture within organizations, moving away from a narrow focus on short-term financial gains towards a more holistic and sustainable approach to business. By prioritizing ethical behavior, stakeholder engagement, and responsible business practices, organizations can create value for society while also driving long-term profitability and growth. In doing so, they can contribute to building a more inclusive, equitable, and sustainable future for all.

Questions:

1. *How can organizations integrate ethical decision-making into their business practices? Discuss specific frameworks or models that can guide leaders in making ethical choices,*

particularly in complex situations.

2. *What are the key principles of corporate social responsibility (CSR), and how can companies balance profit-making with their obligations to stakeholders, including the community and the environment? Provide examples of successful CSR initiatives.*

3. *Describe the challenges of making decisions under conditions of uncertainty. What strategies can leaders use to make informed and effective decisions when faced with incomplete or ambiguous information?*

4. *What is groupthink, and how can it negatively impact decision-making within teams? Discuss strategies that leaders can employ to prevent groupthink and encourage diverse perspectives and critical thinking.*

5. *Explain the concept of behavioral decision-making and how cognitive biases can influence the decisions of individuals and groups. Provide examples of common biases and suggest ways to mitigate their impact in organizational decision-making processes.*

Acknowledgement

We extend our heartfelt gratitude to all those who contributed to the creation and completion of this book. Our sincere appreciation goes to the researchers, practitioners, and educators whose insights have enriched these pages. We also thank our colleagues and mentors for their guidance and support throughout this endeavor.

www.ingramcontent.com/pod-product-compliance
Lightning Source LLC
LaVergne TN
LVHW070228170826
845679LV00035B/1869

* 9 7 9 8 8 9 4 4 6 7 5 3 5 *